HOOSIER VIGILANTES

HOOSIER VIGILANTES

FRONTIER JUSTICE AND THE EVOLUTION OF LAW ENFORCEMENT

ROBERT BOWLING

Published by The History Press
Charleston, SC
www.historypress.com

First published 2024

Manufactured in the United States

ISBN 9781467157223

Library of Congress Control Number: 2024941844

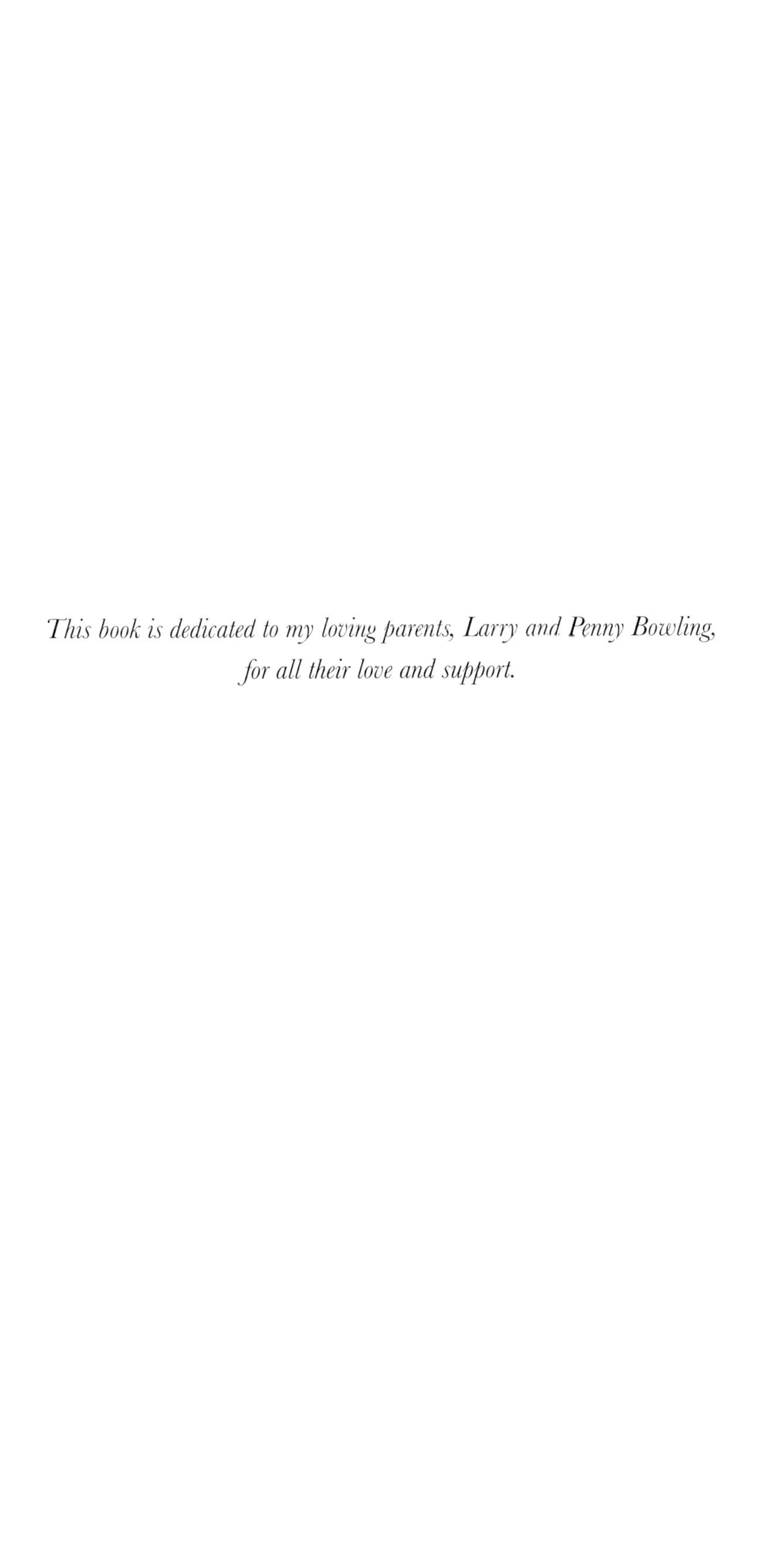

This book is dedicated to my loving parents, Larry and Penny Bowling,
for all their love and support.

CONTENTS

ACKNOWLEDGEMENTS

I would like to thank those who assisted me in writing this book. I am especially grateful to Evan Miller of the Ramsay Archival Center at Wabash College for helping with the Horse Thief Detective Association, Dorothy Richards of the Jackson County History Center for help with the Reno Gang, Karen Schwartz with the Harrison County Historical Society for help researching the White Caps and Don Flick with the Indiana German Heritage Society for helping me with previous history projects. I would like to thank IMPD historian Patrick Pearsey; Shelly Triol, curator at the Indiana State Police Museum; the Officer Down Memorial Page; and Darcy Maulsby for helping to acquire the many photographs featured in the book.

I would also like to extend my gratitude to a fellow teacher, Zach Burkhart. Our shared carpool rides to school provided the perfect setting for in-depth discussions about the book. Zach's unique perspective often led to new insights, prompting me to revisit the manuscript and make necessary changes. His contributions were instrumental in shaping this book, and I am truly thankful for his support and dedication.

INTRODUCTION

In the 1970s and '80s, the crime rate in New York City skyrocketed amid the crack epidemic. The murder rate peaked in 1990 with 2,245 murders, the highest on record. That same year, there were more than 500,000 police complaints, 3,000 rapes and more than 100,000 robberies.[1] Riding the NYC subway had become a frightful experience. A young group of unarmed teenagers called the Guardian Angels attempted to curb the violence through organized patrols.

On December 22, 1984, Bernhard Goetz shot four men on an NYC subway train after they attempted to rob him. In 1981, Goetz had been robbed while on the subway. The police detained Goetz for six hours while the accused was released after two and a half hours. He applied for a concealed handgun permit but was denied. He eventually got a gun while in Florida. After shooting the four men, he fled to Vermont, eventually returning to NYC to surrender to the police. The first grand jury refused to indict him on attempted murder charges, but a second grand jury did. At trial, he was found guilty of illegally possessing a loaded firearm outside his home but was acquitted of attempted murder.[2] The media dubbed him the "Subway Vigilante," and he quickly became one of the most famous vigilantes in American history.

America's history of vigilantism dates back to before the country was founded. In 1773, the British Parliament imposed a series of taxes on the American colonies to help pay its outstanding debt. This angered the colonists, who were subjected to taxation without representation in

Parliament. On December 16, at Griffin's Wharf in Boston, angry colonists dumped 342 chests of tea into the Boston Harbor. Commonly known as the Boston Tea Party, this was the first major act of defiance against England, and it became a rallying cry for independence.[3]

In 1786, another, more violent incident occurred in Massachusetts, known as Shays's Rebellion. Farmers who had fought in the Revolutionary War had received little to no compensation and struggled to make ends meet. Daniel Shays led a group of 600 men to shut down the courts in Springfield. They tried to use peaceful means to get their complaints heard. It eventually escalated when 1,200 men stormed the Springfield Armory, leading to a military confrontation. The incident left 2 men dead and 20 wounded.[4] This was just the beginning of vigilantism in America.

Defining vigilantism is a lot more complicated than it sounds. Merriam-Webster defines a vigilante as a member of a volunteer committee organized to suppress and punish crime when the processes of law are viewed as inadequate.[5] A more common definition is "taking the law into one's own hands." Throughout history, vigilantism has taken on many different forms. Because of this, political scientists have tried to come up with a broad definition to compare across time and space.

There is no consensus on a definition because of the biases among the various disciplines trying to define it. Political scientists view vigilantism as a subtype of political violence,[6] while criminologists see vigilantism in a more favorable and noble light. Actions by vigilantes are viewed as acts of good citizenship that play a key role in establishing social order.[7]

While scholars and political scientists still grapple with how to define vigilantism, so does almost everyone else. Many groups normally identified as vigilantes refuse to think of themselves as such. That is probably due to the negative connotation that the word *vigilante* invokes, while its derivatives, *vigil*, and *vigilance*, are usually considered positive.

America's popular culture shapes society's perception of a vigilante. Children are exposed to vigilantism through comic books and superheroes at a young age. Popular characters such as Batman, the Punisher and Ghost Rider reinforce the idea that the current system is not enough to protect us. DC Comics has a superhero aptly named Vigilante.

Television is filled with examples of vigilantism. *Knight Rider*, *The A-Team* and *The Equalizer* were hit shows based on people taking the law into their own hands, either in conjunction with or against law enforcement. In the 1970s, cinema glorified vigilantism with the popular *Dirty Harry* and *Death Wish* series. The *Los Angeles Times* reported, "Vigilante vengeance was the cinematic theme of the decade, flourishing in the more respectable precincts of the new American cinema even as it fueled numerous exploitation flicks."[8] Vigilante movies have been on the rise recently, with movies like *Law Abiding Citizen*, *Walking Tall* and *Rambo: Last Blood*.

Vigilante justice is driven by a desire to restore the sociopolitical order to a previous level of stability. Political instability is driven by various factors—crime, demographic shifts, government corruption, immigration, economics—and it falls on the vigilante groups to maintain societal values against those who they believe are seeking to destroy their world.[9] Participants are motivated by a fear of victimization, revenge or frustration with the criminal justice system.[10] This is evident by the many different vigilante groups patrolling the U.S. southern border from what appears to be a lack of border security and immigration enforcement by the federal government. Groups such as the Arizona Border Recon, Veterans on Patrol and United People of America have taken it upon themselves to combat illegal immigration and the illicit drug trade.[11]

While some vigilantism is considered to be connected with racism and political extremism, other forms take on a more noble cause. Vigilantism has come to be accepted when people feel that the government can no longer offer them the security and safety they desire. Protection becomes a matter of self-responsibility. Neighborhood Watches are one of the oldest crime prevention programs in history, tracing their origins back to colonial times. People within the community took on the responsibility of providing security against outsiders. Modern Neighborhood Watches began to form shortly after the brutal rape and murder of Kitty Genovese on March 13, 1964. She was murdered outside her Queens, New York apartment building while allegedly thirty-eight people watched, and no one intervened or called the police.[12] In the wake of the murder, local communities formed Neighborhood Watches. In 1972, the National Sheriff's Association made it more formal by creating the U.S. Neighborhood Watch program. Today, there are over twenty thousand local Neighborhood Watch programs and more than fifty thousand informal programs.[13]

Vigilantism grew in response to a lack of law enforcement. Early law enforcement officers were mostly untrained, uneducated men who were usually outnumbered. It was not a full-time job, and they were most often paid by fees levied by the court. Jurisdictional issues prevented officers from pursuing criminals beyond their borders. It wasn't until the early 1900s that law enforcement started to become professionalized. August Vollmer, known as the father of modern policing, introduced many police reforms. As police chief of Berkeley, California, he required officers to have college degrees, created a motorized police force, trained officers in marksmanship and created the first centralized police records system. He also pushed for greater diversity among the officers. He established a criminal justice program at UC–Berkeley, but it was Indiana University that became the first college in the United States to make criminal justice an academic field when the Institute of Criminal Law and Criminology was established in 1935.[14]

Slowly, law enforcement evolved from a corrupt, unorganized system into an organized profession with ethics, codes of conduct and professional standards. Vigilantism continues to exist, and it has become intertwined with law enforcement. This book will discuss the various vigilante groups that have existed in Indiana and how they helped shape modern law enforcement throughout the state.

CHAPTER 1

VIGILANCE COMMITTEES

Beginning around the 1820s, communities throughout the United States began to form vigilance committees as a form of private law enforcement. The ability of the government to enforce law and order proved inadequate, and the responsibility fell on those living in the community. These committees were often quasi-formal associations organized at the county or township level. Occasionally they would form partnerships with groups in adjoining counties or towns. They usually had a constitution outlining membership, dues and the process of arresting criminals. The group aimed to keep watch over the community and enforce the law in lieu of the state. These vigilantes did not see themselves as opponents of the state but rather as defenders of a legitimate form of political authority that existing institutions could not provide.[15]

Vigilance committees used the most fundamental American political principle to justify their actions: the right of the people to govern themselves. In addition to maintaining law and order, these groups formed for other reasons. In the South, they helped to track runaway slaves, while in the North, they assisted slaves in their escape through the Underground Railroad. One such group was the Philadelphia Vigilance Committee, operating between 1837 and 1852, which provided food, rest and transportation to runaway slaves.[16] Some formed to protect themselves against horse thieves, counterfeiters and all types of ruffians.

San Francisco's vigilance committee was the largest in the United States, with more than six thousand members at its peak. First formed in 1851 at the height of the gold rush, it served as a defense to the community against murderers, thieves and rapists who flooded the city. Its members acted as law enforcement officers and maintained a parallel justice system, including lynching and deportation. A gang of criminals from Australia known as the "Sydney Ducks" terrorized the city, resulting in four of them being executed. In 1856, the committee was formed again in response to corruption within the judicial system, which allowed murderers to go free. Today, the 1856 committee remains the best-organized and most successful example of resistance to an established government, along with being the most controversial.[17]

Perhaps Indiana's most famous vigilance committee was seen in Jackson County in the late 1860s. The Jackson County Vigilance Committee was also called the Scarlet Mask Society, which corresponded with their disguise. Merchants and farmers formed the committee amid mounting fear of lawlessness among the citizenry brought on by four brothers: Frank, John, Simeon and William Reno. Together with their associates, they introduced the country to a new crime: train robbery.

Long before the automobile, the train revolutionized travel in the United States. Maryland and South Carolina were the first states to build railroads in the 1830s. By 1850, there were more than nine thousand miles of track throughout the eastern states. In 1851, the railroad crossed the Mississippi River, and boomtowns were settled along its path. With these new towns, crime followed, as it attracted drifters and all sorts of other criminals. There was no railroad police at the time, and local law enforcement couldn't meet the challenge. The responsibility fell on vigilante groups to meet the growing threat.[18]

In 1857, the Ohio and Mississippi Railroad (O&M) was completed connecting Cincinnati with St. Louis. Construction began in 1854 and was finally completed on April 18, 1857, when the last spike was hammered at Mitchell, Indiana. Completion of the railroad was delayed due to the construction of two tunnels near Mitchell. Jackson County had three stops along the route: Seymour, Brownstown and Medora.[19] While Jesse James and his band of outlaws robbed banks, the Reno brothers focused their sights on the railroad. This group would be responsible for carrying out the first peacetime train robbery in the United States.

The Reno family grew up in Rockford, a small town north of Seymour. In addition to the four Reno brothers, they had a sister, Laura, and another brother, Clint, aptly nicknamed "Honest Clint" to differentiate him from his brothers. Although raised in a religious household, the Reno brothers turned to a life of crime at an early age. During the Civil War, they became bounty jumpers. People could pay someone to take their place in the war. The Reno brothers would collect the bounty and then either fail to enlist or desert after they did. They did this numerous times using different names.[20]

After the war, the Reno brothers operated their headquarters out of the Radar Hotel in Seymour, robbing guests along with making counterfeit currency.[21] Recognizing that banks transferred their money by train, the Reno brothers turned their attention to the railroad, as it provided a more substantial payday. On October 6, 1866, John Reno, Simeon Reno and Frank Sparks boarded the eastbound Adams Express Company train at Seymour. Three masked gunmen made off with $12,000 ($227,000 in 2023). The first recorded peacetime train robbery took less than a few minutes to complete.[22]

Unbeknownst to the Reno brothers, the Adams Express Company was under the protection of the Pinkerton Detective Agency in Chicago. Allan Pinkerton, America's first "private eye," created the first private detective agency in the United States around 1850. He first gained national recognition for protecting President-elect Abraham Lincoln as he traveled to Washington, D.C., and he would go on to become chief of intelligence for the Union during the Civil War.[23]

On September 28, 1867, Michael Collins and Walker Hammond carried out a copycat robbery blamed on the Reno Gang. The Renos, not liking competition, had their rivals arrested and sentenced. The Reno Gang had confined their criminal activities to Indiana but decided to branch out. They went to Gallatin, Missouri, and robbed the treasurer's office at the Daviess County Courthouse of $23,618 in cash and bonds.[24]

With John Reno being positively identified, Pinkerton tracked him back to Seymour. Knowing that Seymour was filled with corrupt officials and a populace terrified of the Reno brothers, he devised a plan to capture John. He placed his assistant undercover at the train station to report on John's whereabouts. With a half-dozen Missouri citizens and the Daviess County sheriff, John was seized and transported back to Missouri to stand trial. He protested that he had been kidnapped, but the court disagreed with him. He was sentenced to twenty-five years in the Missouri Penitentiary.[25]

This was the first time that a Reno had been made to answer for their crimes. John was considered the brains of the operation, so now it fell on his other three brothers. In 1868, they went on a crime spree in Iowa, raiding multiple treasurers' offices. They were arrested by Pinkerton detectives but escaped from the jail on April 1 before they could be tried. Upon their escape, they wrote "April Fool" above the hole in the wall.

The gang returned to Seymour to plan their biggest robbery to date. On May 22, 1868, the last train of the night left Jeffersonville heading north and made a refueling stop at Marshfield in Scott County, about seventeen miles south of Seymour. The train arrived at around 11:00 p.m. Twelve masked men overpowered the crew as the train took on supplies. They uncoupled the engine from the rest of the train and took it to Seymour. One of the crew fired on the bandits, but his shots missed. He was found barely alive after he was beaten with pistols and crowbars and thrown from the train.[26]

The outlaws broke into the safe and made away with $96,000 ($2 million in 2023) in cash and bonds. They stopped the train about six miles south of Seymour, and some fled to Indianapolis and others to Windsor, Ontario. Another train robbery was committed on July 10 near Brownstown by other gang members who had stayed in Seymour. The community was fed up with the terrorizing by a handful of bandits, and the Jackson County Vigilance Committee was formed to end it. The *New York Tribune* commented on the state of affairs in Jackson County that vigilance committees were part of the natural order in a society. When crime is rampant, law officers are inattentive to their duties and judges are corrupt, citizens must take the law into their own hands. The only way to prevent this is to enforce the laws and purify the courts, it noted.[27]

The gang members who were involved in the July 10 robbery were John Moore, Henry Jerrell, Frank Sparks, Val Elliott, Charlie Rosenberry and Theodore Clifton. Unbeknownst to them, they were walking into a trap, as Pinkerton detectives were waiting for them. Everyone except for Clifton boarded the train, while he stayed back with the horses. A gun battle broke out on the train, and all five bandits were wounded. They were still able to escape, except for Elliott. He would eventually tell detectives the location of his partners. Clifton and Rosenberry were arrested the next day and taken to the jail in Seymour. On the night of July 20, the three bandits were being transferred by train to the county jail in Brownstown. One hundred people wearing scarlet masks stopped the train about three miles west of Seymour. The masked men took the prisoners and immediately hanged them on a nearby tree. This was the first act of retributive justice committed by the vigilance committee. Although they lacked the state authority to carry out this execution, they were not deterred.[28]

The day after the lynchings, Jerrell, Moore and Sparks were found in Coles County, Illinois. After they were brought to Seymour by train, they would be transferred to Browntown. Pinkerton secretly transferred them by using a wagon instead of a train. That didn't work, as a large group of masked men seized the wagon and the prisoners at almost the same exact spot as the other three. On July 25, they were lynched on the same tree. While the tree is long gone, the area is now called Hangman's Crossing.[29]

On July 27, William and Simeon Reno were arrested in Indianapolis. Concerned that the vigilance committee would go after them, the National Guard was called out to protect the prisoners during a preliminary hearing in Scott County. They were then taken to Floyd County to await trial in the jail in New Albany. Frank Reno and Charles Anderson were eventually arrested in Windsor, Ontario.[30]

Reno and Anderson were charged with robbery and assault with the intent to kill, which made their crime extraditable. Their attorneys argued that delivering Reno and Anderson to the United States would result in almost certain death, as six gang members had already been executed without a trial. Secretary of State William H. Seward and the president of the Adams Express assured the Canadian authorities that Reno and Anderson would have a fair and impartial trial and be protected from lynching parties. If they were found innocent, they would be returned to Canada. Reno and Anderson were extradited into the custody of Pinkerton. They were taken by boat to Cleveland and then by train to New Albany, where they joined William and Simeon Reno.[31]

On the night of December 11, about seventy-five men of the vigilance committee boarded a train from Seymour to Jeffersonville. They took another train to New Albany, arriving at the Pearl Street station around 3:00 a.m. Armed with revolvers and clubs, they surrounded the jail. They seized Deputy Luther Whitten, who was on guard outside. His feet and arms were bound, and he was carried into the jail and placed in a chair.[32]

The masked group then went to the sleeping quarters of Sheriff Thomas Fullenlove and his wife. The sheriff, awakened by the noise, opened the door as the committee entered. They demanded the keys, but the sheriff refused and told him that they would have to shoot him first. Fullenlove escaped from the building through a window but was shot in the arm as he made it to the street. The mob caught him, striking him a few times with the butt of a pistol, and carried him back inside the jail. They locked the sheriff, his wife and the guards in a cell while retrieving the Reno brothers and Anderson from their cells.[33]

The jail was divided into two tiers; the upper tier contained iron pillars from which the group intended to hang them. Simeon was the first to be hanged after receiving a blow to the head, with a stream of blood flowing down his face. Charles Anderson was next, and the wounds on his face showed that he did not go easily. Frank followed after receiving a deep wound behind the ear, possibly made with a slingshot. William was the last to hang, touching his brother Frank as he died. The mob, having completed their job, left the jail and boarded a train back to Seymour. The sheriff estimated that it took them less than five minutes to seize the jail and hang the prisoners.[34]

Opinions were mixed on the lynchings of the vigilance committee. Some applauded their heroic actions for finally ending the Reno brothers' legacy of terror. The *New Albany Commercial* newspaper commended the vigilance committee and believed that their defiance of the law should be excused. Those who disagreed believed that the rest of the country would consider Indiana lawless and bloodthirsty.[35] Their actions against the sheriff proved that they were no better than the Reno Gang. Canada was outraged after the United States broke its promise. Although few had sympathies for the Reno Gang, their execution without a trial was a disgrace to the nation. They believed that every American should be ashamed and that the government should end vigilance committees and work to instill faith in the judicial system.[36]

The Jackson County Vigilance Committee continued to enforce the laws even after the legislature attempted to curb its influence by punishing members of such committees.[37] Vigilance committees spread to other counties, and breaking into jails to steal prisoners became the norm. The Reno brothers' only sister, Laura, brought their bodies back home, and they were buried at Seymour's city cemetery. Charlie Anderson was buried in New Albany. John was released from the Missouri Penitentiary after serving ten years. He returned to Seymour, but seven years later, he was sentenced to three years in the Indiana State Prison for counterfeiting. While some questioned the vigilance committee's actions, they were successful in purging the evil from Seymour, and it went on to become a thriving city and a model town of Indiana.[38]

CHAPTER 2

KNIGHTS OF THE GOLDEN CIRCLE

During the Civil War, a secret society existed that sought to preserve and expand slavery. The Knights of the Golden Circle, formed in 1854 by George W.L. Bickley of Cincinnati, attempted to create new proslavery states in Central America and the Caribbean through annexation. The goal was to create a slaveholding empire extending sixteen geographical degrees or 1,200 miles from its center in Havana, Cuba. This "Golden Circle" would encompass the southern United States, the West Indies, Mexico and Central America, along with Colombia and Venezuela.[39]

It had enormous support in the southern states for its proslavery stance, but it also gained the support of the northern states, as they were concerned about the growing power of the federal government. The ideological differences between the North and South widened with the onset of the Civil War. The Northern states felt that the war was a mistake and that the growing power of the federal government would lead to tyranny. Most of the Golden Circle's Northern support came from Copperheads, a faction of Union Democrats who opposed the Civil War and wanted a peace settlement with the Confederacy.[40]

The Golden Circle was estimated to have had more than 500,000 members in the United States during the war. Between the Northern states of Kentucky, Illinois, Ohio and Missouri, Indiana had the largest membership, between 75,000 and 100,000. That was somewhat ironic, considering that Indiana was the first of the country's western states to mobilize for the war and had voted to remain with the Union. It was most active in southern Indiana, with its first chapters formed in Washington, Orange and Martin Counties.[41]

In each state, the organization had a headquarters or "temple." Indiana had two temples, in Indianapolis and Vincennes. Chapters were referred to as "castles." The group communicated through secret hand signs, grips and words. With members of the organization fighting against one another, they had a signal to remind one another of their obligation and not injure one another on the battlefield. Meetings were usually held in the woods or in abandoned buildings. Only Democrats could join, and youths as young as sixteen could be initiated into the order. Members had to pass through three degrees, which began with militarization, learning the principles and teachings and then culminated with the organization's true purpose.[42] The organization encouraged members to resist the draft, desert from the Union army and actively support the Confederacy.[43]

As it was a paramilitary organization, the leaders held military rank titles. Harrison H. Dodd founded the Golden Circle in Indiana and served as its supreme commander. Horace Heffren from Salem, Indiana, served as the deputy commander. Indiana was divided into four military districts under the command of Major Generals John C. Walker, William Bowles, Lambden Milligan and Andrew Humphreys. These individuals, along with a secretary and treasurer, formed the supreme council that oversaw the activities within each state.[44]

In 1863, the organization changed its name to the Order of American Knights and, the following year, changed it again to the Order of the Sons of Liberty. Some states had alternate names, such as Peace Organization in Illinois, Star Organization in Kentucky and American Organization in Missouri. Outside the organization, its members referred to themselves as "Butternuts"—a term that was used to describe proslavery settlers from Southern states who inhabited the southern parts of Ohio, Indiana and Illinois.[45]

Of the states that supported the Union, Indiana's Sons of Liberty proved to be the most troublesome. That was especially true for Indiana governor Oliver P. Morton, a staunch supporter of Lincoln who thwarted an assassination attempt by members of the order. The assassination plot resulted in a military tribunal, and the case would be appealed to the U.S. Supreme Court.

The plot began in 1864 as Clement Vallandigham, a U.S. representative from Ohio, became the supreme commander of the Sons of Liberty. After losing reelection in 1862, Vallandigham gave a series of speeches criticizing

Lincoln and the war and expressing his opposition to abolitionism. Lincoln had suspended *habeas corpus* and made any discouraging statements about the war and the draft punishable under martial law. Vallandigham fled to Canada, attempting to form a Northwest Confederacy consisting of Illinois, Indiana, Ohio and Kentucky, allied with the Southern Confederacy. The plan called for the overthrow of state governments and the liberation of Confederate prisoners of war.[46]

A plan was formulated to assassinate Governor Morton, raid the military arsenal in Indianapolis and free the Confederate prisoners of war imprisoned at Camp Morton. The largest of the Union's eight prison camps contained nearly five thousand prisoners. There were also plans to free prisoners from Camp Chase in Columbus, Ohio; Camp Butler in Springfield, Illinois; and Camp Douglas in Chicago. The date of the operation was planned for August 16, but Governor Morton discovered the plan as early as July 29, thanks in large part to a confidential informant.[47]

Felix Grundy Stidger was a Secret Service agent working under the direction of the provost marshal in Kentucky. Stidger was instructed to go undercover to infiltrate the Order. He performed admirably, rising to become the grand secretary in Kentucky. Stidger was made privy to the plans formulated in Indiana to steal and transport the arsenal to Louisville. He reported his findings to General Henry Carrington, who was serving in Indiana as an intelligence officer.[48] It was assumed that the lieutenant governor might have been targeted as well. Under the Indiana Constitution, the secretary of state was next in line of succession. The current secretary, James S. Athon, was a member of the Sons of Liberty, and by installing him as the governor, they would control the state.[49]

General Alvin Peterson Hovey, military commander of the Indiana district, was ordered to arrest the conspirators. Harrison Dodd, Horace Heffren, William Bowles, Lambden Milligan, Andrew Humphreys and Stephen Horsey were arrested. They were each charged with five different offenses: conspiring against the government of the United States, affording aid and comfort to the rebels against the authority of the United States, inciting insurrection, disloyal practices and violations of the laws of war. With the suspension of *habeas corpus*, Hovey convened a military tribunal to try the conspirators.[50]

As the leader of the organization, Dodd was tried first. The military tribunal consisted of nine members—one general, seven colonels and one major—and convened in Indianapolis on September 22, 1864. The trial continued until October 7, when Dodd escaped from custody. He had been confined in a room in an office building. That morning, a rope had been discovered hanging from his window. Dodd fled to Canada. He was tried in absentia and found guilty, sentenced to be hanged.[51]

The other members went on trial on October 21 by the same military tribunal. They were all found guilty except for Heffron. After Heffron agreed to testify against his co-conspirators, the government dropped the charges against him. Although Humphreys was found guilty, he received a most unusual punishment and commutation. The tribunal determined that Humphreys did not take an active part in the insurrection, but his association warranted confinement to hard labor for the duration of the war. However, Hovey commuted this sentence to confinement within the boundaries of Stockton and Wright Townships in Greene County for the duration of the war. Leaving the boundaries of these two townships would violate his parole, and he would be sent to Kentucky to carry out his sentence.[52]

Bowles, Milligan and Horsey were found guilty and sentenced to hang. Their execution was scheduled for May 19, 1865. The same prisoners whom they were accused of trying to release from Camp Morton were forced to build the gallows. Three days before their execution, President Andrew Johnson commuted the sentence of Horsey to life imprisonment in the federal penitentiary in Columbus, Ohio. Milligan's and Bowles's executions were suspended until June 2, when their sentences were commuted to life imprisonment.[53]

Lambden Milligan was not content to hang or serve a life sentence. He appealed his conviction to the circuit court, which had convened on January 2, 1865. The judges were split on whether to release Milligan, and his case was referred to the U.S. Supreme Court. In March 1866, the Supreme Court heard oral arguments. Four attorneys represented Milligan: Joseph E. McDonald; Jeremiah Black, U.S. attorney general under former president James Buchanan; David Dudley Field, whose brother was on the Supreme Court; and future president James A. Garfield, in his first court appearance.

The lawyers for Milligan argued that the military tribunal had no authority to try him because he was a citizen of the United States and Indiana. He was not a citizen of any of the rebellion states, and therefore he was entitled to a trial by jury as provided for in the Constitution. Although Congress upheld Lincoln's suspension of *habeas corpus*, three questions were posed to the court. First, should a writ of *habeas corpus* be issued to Milligan? Second, should Milligan be discharged from custody? And third, did the military tribunal have jurisdiction to try to sentence him?[54]

In a 5 to 4 opinion, the U.S. Supreme Court decided for Milligan, who was ordered to be released. The court ruled that the military had no authority to try him as he was not in the military and was a resident of a state where the civilian courts were still operating. The court also ruled that citizens can only be detained without charges, not tried and sentenced under *habeas corpus*. The case, *Ex Parte Milligan* (1866), ruled that the federal government could not establish military courts to try civilians except when the civilian courts were no longer functioning. The case helped establish the tradition that presidential and military action in times of war had limits.[55]

The U.S. Supreme Court decision wasn't handed down until December 1866. Milligan and his co-conspirators were released after serving nearly eighteen months. Milligan returned home to Huntington, Indiana, and filed a civil lawsuit against Morton, Hovey and the members of the military tribunal for false arrest and imprisonment. He asked for $100,000 in damages.[56] Future president Benjamin Harrison represented the defendants in the case. Milligan was represented by future governor and future vice president Thomas Hendricks, who was rumored to have been a member of the Sons of Liberty. The case was decided in 1871 in favor of Milligan. Because of the law at the time, Milligan was awarded only $5 and court costs.[57]

After the trial in 1864 and the war's end in 1865, the organization dwindled and mostly disappeared. The conspirators returned to Indiana, mostly destitute.[58] After the sentence was overturned, Dodd returned from exile in Canada and settled in Wisconsin. Ironically, he became a Republican in 1872 and served several terms as mayor of Fond du Lac.[59] Milligan, whose name is forever etched in the annals of legal history, died in 1899. He went on to have a successful career as a lawyer but never overcame the financial troubles that arose from his case.[60]

CHAPTER 3

WHITE CAPS

In the early 1870s, a couple in Crawford County was subjected to many atrocities by masked men known as the White Caps. It began shortly after the Civil War when Henry Houghton returned home to Crawford County and joined the White Caps. He was told that the group was focused on stopping horse thieving and counterfeiting. He soon discovered that the group was nothing more than a band of ruffians that inflicted whippings on other human beings. He denounced the group and wanted nothing to do with them.

In 1873, Henry married Nancy, and the White Caps began to wage their personal vendetta against the newly married couple. Twenty masked men and women broke into their house a year into their marriage and took Nancy from her bed. She was stripped naked, tied to a tree and given thirty lashes on her bare back. She was pregnant with their first child, a mere two weeks away. The reason for the beating was that the couple was "not acting right." It was unusual for women to participate in these attacks, and Nancy later testified that they were more brutal than the men. One of the women who beat her had the audacity to come to her house the next day to check on her. It had nothing to do with sympathy but rather with reporting back to the group. The woman was identified because she was still wearing the dress she had worn the night before.

Even after being called out by Nancy, the attacks continued for years, sometimes without warning. Their life of happiness turned into terror. The community socially ostracized them. Every year, they were subjected to some kind of assault. Henry was captured one night and received one hundred lashes, which caused him to faint. He was then tied with a rope and dragged a long distance down the road. He eventually recovered but was told to leave the county. They lived on an eighty-acre farm but soon abandoned it and moved to Leavenworth, three miles away. The whippings continued year after year, usually for some minor offense.

Sometime in the mid-1880s, one of Houghton's children got into an argument with a neighbor's child. Seeing that his son's life was in danger, he fired his revolver, and the bullet struck the neighbor's child in the arm. Although he claimed self-defense, he was sentenced to state prison for three years. It was believed that the years of assaults by the White Caps had made him insane. The case grabbed the attention of Governor Isaac Gray, who believed that Houghton should be in an insane asylum, not prison.

With her husband in prison, Nancy was forced to raise their five children without money. A few people in town tried to help her, but they were condemned and threatened. One citizen went before the county commissioners to request that they give her $1.50 a week for subsistence. They granted the request but soon rescinded it when the White Caps intervened. She was forced to flee Leavenworth after the White Caps threatened her with one hundred lashes. She lived her life in poverty on a riverboat on the Ohio River.[61]

The Houghton case was just one of many cases uncovered by Attorney General Louis T. Michener. In 1888, Governor Isaac Gray sent Michener to investigate the atrocities waged by the White Caps. White Cap activity was mostly confined to the southern counties. He first went to Corydon in Harrison County, the former capital of Indiana. Harrison County had become the center and unofficial headquarters of the White Caps. The organization was so secretive and its members so unknown that it was difficult to prosecute anyone or know their inner workings.[62] The increase in White Cap beatings was also receiving national attention. A reporter with the *Sun* in New York City traveled to Indiana to visit with the White Caps.[63]

HISTORY OF THE WHITE CAPS

The White Caps seem to have originated in the late 1790s in County Kerry, Ireland. A large Irish family, the Whitecaps, took it upon themselves to enforce a moral code in the community. They would take people from their homes and whip them with a cat-o'-nine-tails, a multi-tailed whip used by the Royal Navy and British army for punishment. Similar groups spread throughout Ireland called "whitecaps"—spelled one word, unlike the two-word version in the United States.[64]

It is hard to say when the White Caps first formed, but members' confessions during that period put it as early as 1868. Vigilance committees and horse thief detective companies had been around for decades and were scattered throughout Indiana. In Harrison County, a group called the Regulators enforced the laws and protected law-abiding citizens. The group began to spread to neighboring counties, and eventually, they became the White Caps.[65] Many members formerly belonged to the Knights of the Golden Circle, which was forced to disband in 1863 after a failed attempt to assassinate the Indiana governor.

The White Caps were mostly located in the southern counties, notably Crawford, Perry, Harrison, Martin, Washington, Orange and DuBois. This was attributable to two reasons. The terrain of these southern counties was vastly different than in the north. The terrain was beautiful and romantic, with rolling hills, caves and hidden rivers. But as beautiful as it was, it was not easily accessible. There were few railroads in this area, and until 1886, the county seats of Orange and Harrison Counties could not be reached by train. The only road through the territory was treacherous, meandering through the rolling hills.[66]

The northern counties were more heavily populated than the southern ones and had more railroad access. While the terrain in the south was not ideal for settlers, it was perfect for criminals. The Ohio River attracted thieves who mostly lived on boats. They would rob farmers along the river, stealing everything from food to chickens. It was much easier to terrorize people along a waterway than by railroad. Kentucky afforded an easy escape route should the criminals be pursued. This lawlessness gave rise to the White Caps.[67]

The White Caps closely resembled the Ku Klux Klan of the South. In 1888, a reporter for New York's *Sun* newspaper was given exclusive access to the group, which had garnered national attention. Their regalia was described in detail. They wore white paper foolscaps, white paper masks and coats made from coffee sacks. The coats were made by cutting holes for the arms and the heads. The caps resembled a dunce cap that disorderly students would have to wear in school. It was merely a sheet of paper rolled so that it came to a point at the top and flared out over the skull at the bottom. The white mask was nothing more than a sheet of paper with holes cut out for the eyes and nose. Twine was used to hold the mask to the head. It was evident to the reporter that women had no role in making the costume, as there was no sewing, and the outfit looked simple and childish.[68]

The White Caps did their work by night on horseback. Each man carried a weapon or a shotgun, which was seldom used. Their preferred weapon was the hickory switch, which each man personally picked out. The switches were normally four feet in length. The switches were held over a fire until the bark became scorched. The switch was then twisted from one end to the other. Putting the switch through this process made the switch flexible like rubber, with the strength of rawhide.[69]

The White Caps were secretive and well organized. They had a defined hierarchy, with each "lodge" having a chairman and secretary. The lodge meetings were usually held in abandoned buildings or in sinkholes deep in the forest. Sentinels would be stationed around the meeting site to protect the members from unwanted intrusion by nonmembers. The organization utilized secret signs, grips and passwords to further keep out those who tried to infiltrate the organization.[70]

The White Caps' initiation process was designed so that the lodge could control its members. The death oath was the first step in the initiation, which required the prospective member to recite an oath while on their knees looking down the barrel of a gun. The initiate would be required to deposit $200 in the lodge to ensure that its members were wealthy enough to join the group. In addition to the death oath, the initiate would take another oath that required him to admit that he had committed some form of crime. This would be done voluntarily and certified before a magistrate. The certified oath would be kept in the lodge before the initiate could learn any of the organization's secrets. This oath forced the initiate to admit that they were a criminal, and the lodge used it as a source of blackmail if the member ever tried to leave the organization or divulge its secrets.[71]

After the lodge received the initiate's oath, the person was admitted to full membership. Lodge meetings were called for by the chairman whenever there was someone in the community who needed to be warned or whipped—delegates at the meeting volunteered to carry out the chairman's orders. Members were not obligated to go on raids. However, if they volunteered, they were expected to follow the captain's orders. Killing was discouraged and only allowed during self-defense. If the plan were foiled, for whatever reason, they would attempt it again until they were successful. Along with the oaths, members made pledges to their brothers. If a member was arrested, other members were expected to go to court and try to get on the jury. If a member was wounded while on a raid, they must be shot. "Dead men tell no tales" was once a password within the organization.[72]

In the beginning, the actions of the White Caps were seen as noble. They were applauded for their efforts to rid the community of criminals. Some of their accolades included: "Best thing ever gotten up in the state," "saves the state untold fees," "punishes the evil-doer summarily" and "a greater terror to him than all the courts and jails."[73] In addition to removing horse thieves and counterfeiters, they also enacted their own code of morality. Those who were subjected to whippings were wife-beaters, drunkards, adulterers, women having children out of wedlock or just anyone with loose morals or being lazy.[74] One man was whipped for failing to get his wife firewood.[75]

But public opinion began to change when the White Caps began using their power to wage personal vendettas or engage in whippings without any proof of wrongdoing. In Leavenworth, a fifty-year-old man and his eighteen-year-old stepdaughter were accused of sexual immorality, of which there was no proof. They were both pulled from their residence and tied to a tree. She was given fifty lashes and he seventy-five; both fainted from the pain. After the punishment, they were given twenty days to leave the county. They were confined to their beds for two to three weeks. The whipping of a defenseless girl with no evidence aroused extreme bitterness within the community.[76]

There was no justification for the whippings inflicted by the White Caps. The "crimes" did not justify the level of brutality inflicted on victims. One man was lashed for not providing for his sick wife, one received twenty lashes for using profanity, another was lashed for not paying debts on time, one man had his wrists broken for not loaning his neighbor seed for the farm, one was whipped for not working and one man was punished for visiting with an unmarried woman.[77]

Attorney General Michener's investigation revealed that it was almost impossible to prosecute the White Caps. Some of the most prominent men in society were members, including judges, prosecutors, wealthy businessmen and politicians. White Cap members served on the juries, ensuring that no member would ever be convicted. In 1886, nine supposedly White Cap members were charged with assault and battery. Seven of them were tried and acquitted. The prosecutor dropped the charges against the others for lack of evidence. Those same nine were charged with conspiracy to commit murder against two individuals, and the charges were all dismissed.

Although the attorney general led the investigation, it was made clear that he lacked any authority to enforce the law regarding the White Caps.

Indiana law only allowed the attorney general to get involved in criminal cases when they reached the Indiana Supreme Court. Enforcement of the laws and prosecution of criminals was the sole responsibility of the local courts. However, when the administration of justice became corrupt, holding the White Caps accountable was nearly impossible. The White Caps operated with near impunity with no fear of prosecution.

The attorney general put most of the responsibility on the citizens within these counties to enact change, as they were the ones who serve on the juries and had to be vocal in their condemnation of the White Caps. During their existence, White Caps drove citizens out of the county and state, brutally whipped citizens and beat helpless women and elderly persons until they almost died. They flaunted their power by publishing their whipping notices in the newspapers.[78] Papers such as the *Jasper Courier*, *Crawford Democrat* and *English News* were supportive of the White Caps, while the *Crawford Republican* was in stark opposition.[79] The White Caps lowered property values by as much as half. There was no trust within the community, which was considered essential for a good society.

THE CONRADS

In August 1893, an attack by the White Caps backfired disastrously, taking the lives of five of its members. It also showed that the White Caps were less invincible than they thought. The Conrads lived in Harrison County, almost inaccessible from the county seat, Corydon, sixteen miles away. Their house was on the banks of Mosquito Creek, a mile away from any inhabited place. Only a small wagon road, almost impassable, led to their home.[80] The family consisted of the father, Edward; his wife; and their children, Fannie, William and Samuel. A few weeks earlier, Edward had been found dead at his home. His skull had been fractured, and a bloody piece of timber lay beside him. His two sons, William and Samuel, were charged with their father's murder.[81]

The sons had a good reputation within the community. They were quiet, hardworking, never drank and always paid their debts. Edward was the exact opposite. He was prone to anger, quarreled with everyone and was known to abuse his family. He beat his sons and occasionally kicked his wife and daughter. At their preliminary trial, the sons claimed that a dispute arose while chopping wood. Their father fell against the outside stove and died from his injuries. Their mother defended her boys, and with no other evidence, the prosecutor had no choice but to dismiss the case.[82]

Furious that the Conrad brothers were not tried, the White Caps planned an attack with the intention of lynching them. Shortly after midnight on August 6, nearly sixty White Caps arrived at their cabin. The brothers had been forewarned and were waiting for them. They hid underneath the porch. Holes had been dug into the flooring to allow the muzzle of their rifles to protrude out. The Conrads fired their weapons as the White Caps stepped onto the porch. Two men died instantly, while three more were found hundreds of yards away several hours later. While the White Caps tended to their wounded, the Conrad family fled.[83]

The Conrad family fled across the Ohio River to Kentucky. The White Caps spread across the county all day on Sunday, looking for missing members and checking on wounded ones. The Conrad brothers planned to kill anyone associated with their trial. After their mother and sister were safe, the brothers crossed back into Indiana. Fear spread throughout the county as riderless horses were discovered. The Conrads were laying an ambush, and it was believed that they had killed another six members. On Monday, after the White Caps spent the majority of the day burying their dead, the other members went to the Conrad home and burned it down.[84]

The Conrads succeeded in scaring the White Caps and paralyzed them with fear. The community was standing behind the Conrads, believing that they were innocent. They hoped that the Conrads had dealt the death blow to the White Caps. The sheriff refused to arrest the Conrads or make any attempt to locate them, justifying their actions as self-defense. White Cap members dared not defend their actions for fear of reprisal.[85] It took the strength and courage of two young men to humble an organization that had operated with almost impunity for years.

The White Caps were definitely stunned, but they didn't back down. Over the years, the White Caps had begun to expand into neighboring counties. White Cap activity had gotten so bad in Monroe County, home to Indiana University, that the governor threatened to move the university to another part of the state if the local authorities couldn't stop it.[86] Although the White Caps were mostly confined to areas south of Indianapolis, there were incidences of White Cap activity farther north in Lafayette and Muncie.[87] In Fishers, Henry Klepfer was found tied to a tree and whipped. He claimed that it was the work of the White Caps. Klepfer was a drunk and a wife-beater, so it didn't surprise anyone. What alarmed the residents was that White Caps normally didn't go north of Indianapolis. It was later revealed that his wife tied him to the tree after he passed out. Then she beat him the same way he beat her. It was easier for him to blame it on the White Caps than to tell the community that his wife did it.[88]

Every governor since Gray attempted to eradicate the White Caps. In 1889, the legislature finally passed the White Cap law. The law provided that if three or more people wearing masks should enter a house at night and kidnap the occupant for the purpose of "whipping, beating, bruising, or wounding," they would be charged with riotous conspiracy. The charge carried a prison term of no less than two years and no more than ten in prison and a fine of up to $2,000.[89]

In Marion, Ezra Farr was the first to be tried for beating a woman and her daughter under the new law. After forty-eight hours, the jury was deadlocked, 10 to 2, for acquittal.[90] While many White Caps were brought to trial over the years, no one was ever convicted. The law doesn't mean much if the courts can't convict anyone. Things were about to change when, on May 4, 1911, Harvey McFarley was dragged out of his Bloomington home and whipped by fifteen masked men. McFarley put up a fight, and during the struggle, he knocked the masks off a few of them and recognized their faces. He said that the attack was politically motivated and based on a personal disagreement.[91]

The investigation resulted in the arrest of seven people. Previously, all defendants were tried together, and getting a conviction was difficult. In this case, the prosecutor tried each member separately. Tobe Snoddy was the first to go on trial and became the first White Cap to be convicted under the 1899 law.[92] Silas Adams was the next and only other person convicted. The convictions signaled that the days of using "Old Alibi" to escape justice were over. Forty years of immunity from the law came crashing down.[93]

While Bloomington recorded the first conviction under the 1899 law, it also saw the last recorded incident of "white capping" in June 1928. The suspects were two married couples and a single woman. They had objected to Warren Hamm taking his baby to relatives in Owen County after his wife had become deranged and threatened to kill the young child. The men wore masks, while the three women dressed up as men. They broke into the home and beat Hamm and his brother. They were all arrested and fined twenty-five dollars.[94] The demise of the White Caps would coincide with the rise of another group in Indiana, the Ku Klux Klan.

CHAPTER 4

HORSE THIEF DETECTIVE ASSOCIATION

Horse theft is one of the oldest crimes in the world, dating back to the medieval period. Long before the automobile, the horse was the primary mode of transportation. In addition to personal uses, there were commercial purposes for the horse as a farm implement and as a source of income. Stealing a horse could severely affect a person's ability to travel or make money for their family. Horse theft was a capital crime punishable by death in many societies worldwide.

The Native Americans were the first to introduce horse thieving in the United States. They had turned it into an art form using different techniques to disguise the horse. Being a successful horse thief was considered a badge of honor.[95] Because horse stealing had become such a problem, the United States was forced to sign a peace treaty in 1789 with various tribes to stop it. Any horses stolen by the Native Americans could be reclaimed by the rightful owner, regardless of which hands they passed through. It also applied to any citizen of the United States who stole a horse from the Native Americans.[96] The treaties with the Native Americans were often broken. Shortly after the Civil War, horse thieving increased as the frontier expanded. Horses were in high demand, fueling the need for stealing, and it quickly became the nation's most troublesome crime.[97]

In the 1840s, the Redwood Gang, a horse-stealing group of bandits, terrorized Indiana. They were considered the most powerful and the most feared of any such group. Their base of operations was along the Wabash River in Warren County, just south of Attica, known as Redwood. The group would seek out horses to steal and transport them back to Redwood. Their sphere of activity extended into Warren, Vigo, Vermillion, Fountain, Parke, Tippecanoe and Montgomery Counties, as well as eastern counties in Illinois. Redwood was an ideal spot to carry out their lawless activities because it was sparsely populated. The soil was too broken to cultivate, and no one wanted to raise their families in this part of Indiana.

The twenty-five-member gang was led by a Kentuckian, Isaac Hye, with his son, George, as his lieutenant. His wife and three daughters took on other roles to assist in the gang's activities. In the wilds of Redwood stood cliffs and caves along the Wabash River. Inside one cave, the gang established an underground stable for the horses, which could hold fifty at a time. The natural barriers of the land made it nearly inaccessible for anyone to find them. Only one spot on the Wabash River could be crossed, and that was known only to the gang. It took nearly two years before their headquarters were discovered.[98]

Horse thieving became such a problem that in 1845, three men, John S. Gray, Simeon Osborn and Thomas Hall, organized a group for self-protection. Near the town of Wingate in Montgomery County, the Council Grove Minute Men was officially formed and became the first horse thief detective association organized in the United States.[99] Chapters were formed in the surrounding counties throughout the Wabash Valley. By 1850, chapters had spread into Illinois and Ohio, and the organization was renamed the Wabash Horse-Thief General Detective Association. John Gray served as president of the organization for thirty-eight years. In 1891, at the age of eighty-four, he was granted the lifetime honorary position of "Grand Organizer." He was known for his sterling integrity and was affectionately called "Uncle Saint Gray."

After Isaac Hye shot at two Minute Men as they tried to capture his son, George, a force was mobilized to raid Redwood by all means necessary. Fifty organization members under the command of Captain McKibben and the Vermillion County (Illinois) sheriff entered Redwood. A horse thief who had been captured led the group to the log cabin occupied by the Hyes. Dogs alerted the Redwood Gang to the Minute Men's approach. Everyone escaped except for George and his three sisters, who barricaded themselves in the house, refusing to surrender. The Minute Men fired numerous times into the house. One of the Hye daughters, Suse, opened the door and fired back, striking McKibben, who later died from his wounds. Suse was wounded when the Minute Men shot her nine times. George and his two sisters were found hiding underneath a bed. They were taken to jail and tried within one day. Each was sentenced to ten years in the state penitentiary in Alton, Illinois. They would die of tuberculosis before they were released.[100]

After the raid, the rest of the Redwood Gang went on the run. One horse thief avoided jail time after he agreed to testify against all those who were captured. Although Suse was shot nine times, she recovered from her wounds and ironically filed a civil suit in Fountain County for $25,000. The case was moved to Montgomery County, where Gray was appointed foreman of the jury. Unsurprisingly, Suse lost her case. The horse thief detectives proved to be a success in putting down organized crime, especially in rural areas where lawlessness flourished.[101]

The Indiana legislature recognized that law enforcement was inadequate to protect people from the growing threat of horse thieves and other types of felons. In 1852, the legislature passed an act allowing for the formation of companies of at least ten members, not to exceed one hundred, for the detection and apprehension of horse thieves. The companies would have officers, a constitution and bylaws. The most important feature was that members of these companies were granted constable powers to arrest offenders in accordance with state law.[102] While horse thief companies are considered vigilance committees, their state-granted arrest powers differentiate them from the vigilance committees in southern Indiana that lynched the Reno Gang.

With the law's passage, similar groups began forming around the state. At the same time as the Redwood Gang, a different group of bandits was terrorizing the northern part of Indiana, specifically Noble County. It was a favorable site for bandits, as it was heavily forested, providing great places for hiding. The bandits targeted whites and Native Americans, as there were still some Pottawatomie Indians left in the area. Although there were laws, they were useless because there was no one to enforce them.[103]

In 1856, the LaGrange County Rangers were formed to protect citizens in LaGrange and Noble Counties. According to their preamble, they believed in the doctrine of popular sovereignty. When the enforcement of the law proves to be inadequate for the protection of its citizens, they argued, it is the right of the people to take protection into their own hands. Within a year and a half, thirty-seven companies were operating in Northern Indiana. Most were called Regulators, with a few named after the Horse Thief Detective Association. Other groups had unique names, such as the Noble County Invincibles, Springfield Spies, Eden Police and Self-Protectors at Flint.[104]

The most sensational moment of the Regulators came in 1858 with the execution of Gregory McDougle. McDougle was considered one of the most dangerous criminals in Noble County. Originally from Ontario, Canada, McDougle had started a life of crime at an early age. He settled in Rome City, a small town in Noble County, and continued his evil ways. He confessed to robbing a schoolteacher in Canada and severely beating him. The Regulators claimed that the teacher died of his wounds, and there was a reward for McDougle's capture.[105]

Based on McDougle's confession, the Regulators charged him with murder, although it supposedly occurred in Canada. He was taken to Ligonier and executed by hanging on January 26, 1858. The Regulators' attorney opposed the execution without due process, but the committee overruled him. There were mixed feelings within the community. Some praised the actions of the Regulators, while others opposed taking another human life. The decision also weighed heavily on the members of the committee. But they felt that their "natural and God-given rights had been disregarded and that the arm of the law was too weak to mete out a just retribution to the guilty under the existing state of society."[106] After the execution, the Regulators disbanded.[107]

Horse thief companies continued to grow throughout Indiana over the next few decades. Their powers also increased. In 1885, presidents of horse thief companies could administer official oaths. In 1891, they could pursue into any county in the state and detain a criminal without a warrant or until such time that one can be procured. Sheriffs were still not allowed to pursue outside their county. In 1893, the horse thief companies in Indiana, Illinois and Ohio reorganized to become the National Horse Thief Detective Association (NHTDA). A similar organization, the National Anti-Horse Thief Detective Association, covered Missouri, Kansas, Iowa and Nebraska.[108]

Horse thieving was almost a science. One of the first acts of a horse thief was to remove the horses' shoes so they could not be tracked. Members of the horse thief companies had unique shoes on their horses for identification. They worked in teams, always traveling by night and hiding the horse during the day. They would disguise the horse by dyeing or shearing it, and within two hours, the horse would be almost unrecognizable even to its owner. If the thief were not caught within twelve hours of the theft, they almost certainly escaped punishment.[109]

The NHTDA had political backing, as Indiana governor James Mount was president of the association. Speaking at the national convention in 1893 in Madison, Indiana, Mount stated that he believed there was a growing need for the NHTDA: "Without some co-operation looking to the arrest of the criminal parasites who are too lazy to work and too mean to respect the rights of others, such localities must suffer. Laws upon the statute books against crime are not sufficient to deter criminals. They become effective only when enforced. It is to be earnestly hoped that the good people of Indiana will be aroused to a personal responsibility and see to it that the laws are enforced, and lawlessness suppressed."[110]

There were complaints by farmers that the NHTDA was too concerned with horse thieving and overlooking lesser crimes. In 1906, a smaller organization, the Farmers' Protective Association, was formed that pursued horse thieves and all classes of crimes that annoyed farmers the most. These included chicken thieves, harness thefts and cutting of buggy tires.[111] As the automobile replaced the horse, the NHTDA expanded its responsibilities. Members began to enforce speeding violations within their communities[112] and waged a campaign against automobile parking at night on state highways. They also pursued chicken thieves, robbers and murderers.[113]

In 1907, the county commissioners were granted the power to appoint members of the association as constables within their jurisdiction, and they would be entitled to all of the powers given to constables elected under the law.[114] With no application process, training or background checks, there were many instances of NHTDA members abusing their powers and making false arrests. Horse thief detectives drew the ire of police officers, who viewed them with disdain and contempt. As popular as the organization had become, the tide began to turn against them.

By 1925, there were more than thirty-six thousand NHTDA members in Indiana. Attempts were made in the legislature to curb their influence. A house bill to abolish the NHTDA and replace it with a bonded state constabulary was defeated.[115] Another bill attempted to prevent the abuse of police powers by NHTDA members whose authority had been granted indiscriminately. It proposed that members be state residents for two years (six months in the county where the organization exists), own real estate and post a $1,000 surety bond. It would grant the secretary of state the power to seek information into the character of those seeking membership and deny a charter to association units. Existing chapters would have ninety days to meet the requirements. That bill also failed to gain support.[116]

Tensions boiled over on primary election day in 1925 in Marion County between the Indianapolis police and members of the local NHTDA. Earlier that year, a bill outlawing the carrying of concealed weapons passed. It specifically exempted sheriffs, marshals, police officers and duly appointed police officers. The NHTDA believed that its members were peace officers and thereby exempt from the law. The members also considered that it was their duty to stand watch at the polls.

According to the Indianapolis police, the night before the polls opened, the members of the NHTDA were intimidating Black voters in the neighborhood of Nineteenth and Yandes Streets by driving around and waving their revolvers. They were also passing out political flyers for John Duvall, Republican candidate for mayor. The Black voters were angered, and a riot was averted by the Indianapolis police, but not before at least one NHTDA member was stabbed in the arm. The police ordered the members to go home.

Charles Riddle, head of the Marion County HTDA, and his attorney went to the home of Judge Clinton H. Gavin at 4:30 a.m. to ask for a restraining order. The order prevented the Indianapolis police from interfering with NHTDA members while at the polls. Indianapolis police captain Charles Sumner was outraged by the judge's order. He was heard saying, "To hell with the court's order. I don't give a damn about them. We will lock them all up." The Indianapolis police arrested fifty-five NHTDA members, charging them with carrying concealed weapons and vagrancy. The police also insisted that they had no legal right to guard the polls. The NHTDA turned around and filed warrants against the police officers for assault and battery. The members were eventually released, and Captain Charles Sumner was charged with contempt of court.[117]

According to Judge Gavin, the law passed in 1925 gave peace officers the right to carry weapons, and members of the NHTDA were clearly peace officers. While previous bills to limit the power of horse detectives failed, an unofficial opinion by the state attorney general, Arthur Gilliom, would severely cripple the organization. In his opinion, he ruled that HTDA members can only do what they were created to do: detect and apprehend horse thieves and other felons. Gilliom clarified that "other felons" meant those who are related to horse stealing. He also ruled that the members have no police or constabulary powers. Therefore, if the members are not peace officers, they have no right to carry weapons and may be arrested. County commissioners do not have the right to license them to do so. Members of the NHTDA are part of a voluntary association with no real official status.[118] As for Captain Sumner, he was found guilty of contempt of court and fined seventy-five dollars and seven days in jail, but a later apology wiped the charge from his record.[119]

The Indiana Supreme Court reviewed Attorney General Gilliom's opinion. It ruled that members did have constable powers; however, they were required to submit a $1,000 bond to the state ten days after appointment. Marion County horse thief detectives were not required to post any bonds.[120] Gilliom called on the legislature to repeal the laws that created the HTDA. The organization still drew much support, especially in the rural communities that lacked law enforcement. While horse theft was not much of a problem anymore, chicken thefts cost the farmers of the state nearly $1 million.[121]

Public opinion began to turn against the HTDA when it was revealed that it was being used as a law enforcement arm of the Ku Klux Klan. The Klan was first formed after the Civil War, lasting until 1872. The second era of the Klan began in 1915, and it arrived in Indiana during the early 1920s. At its height, there were 250,000 members in Indiana. They were successful in infiltrating all levels of government. In Muncie, the mayor, prosecuting attorney, chief of police and county commissioners were all rumored to be part of the Klan.[122] Daisy Douglas Barr, vice-chair of the Indiana Republican Party, was the leader of the women's organization within the Klan.[123]

In 1925, D.C. Stephenson, grand dragon of the KKK, was tried for the rape and murder of Madge Oberholtzer, a state employee who ran a program to combat adult illiteracy. After she had been raped and suffered bite marks all over her body, she committed suicide by eating a box of mercury bichloride tablets. Because her suicide resulted from the injuries inflicted on her by Stephenson, he was charged with second-degree murder, rape and kidnapping. The case was moved to Noblesville in Hamilton County on a change of venue.[124]

Stephenson considered himself untouchable. He once declared, "I am the law in Indiana." He had helped Governor Edward Jackson get elected, and it was believed that half of the Indiana General Assembly were Klan members.[125] He assumed that his political influence would save him. Stephenson was found guilty and sentenced to life imprisonment. When he couldn't cash in, he revealed the names of everyone who benefited from the Klan support. Governor Jackson was later indicted for bribery related to Stephenson but was freed on a technicality.[126]

The association of the Klan with the HTDA caused county commissioners to begin to rescind their constable powers. In Vanderburgh County, members of the HTDA included one person in prison for murdering his wife; a few had criminal records, with the most eye-opening being Lee Smith, then grand dragon for the Klan. The Vanderburgh chapter had formed in 1923, around the same time the Klan gained strength.[127] In

South Bend, the St. Joseph County commissioners rescinded the powers of more than eight hundred detectives, as they had been identified as members of the Klan.[128]

While there were most certainly Klan members in the HTDA, there doesn't appear to be any evidence that the organization was working in tandem with the Klan. Attorney General Gilliom launched an investigation to oust the Klan from Indiana and revoke its charter. During the investigation, Klan officials revealed that Stephenson wanted an HTDA chapter that would be affiliated with the Klan. He wanted to exploit the constable powers that were given to the members for his own political gain.[129]

The HTDA tried to distance itself from the Klan by disavowing any links between the two groups.[130] At the 1928 national convention, the organization also underwent a name change. As the automobile had made horse thieves almost obsolete, the organization was renamed the National Detective Association.[131] This possibly could have been a deflection, as the HTDA name had become tainted.

Pressure to abolish the HTDA was gaining steam. Senator John Niblack of Marion County called the detectives a "bunch of shakedown artists." He was the driving force to establish a state police force. Amid the criticism, the association still had supporters. Without a state police force, farmers depended on the horse thief detectives. Some senators dismissed the idea that the HTDA was connected to the Klan or that it was a Klan organization.[132]

Regardless of the support, the writing was on the wall. In 1933, the Indiana legislature passed the Executive Reorganization Act, which officially created the Indiana State Police. The Senate passed the House bill abolishing the HTDA by a 56 to 27 margin. The law also applied to bank vigilantes, private detective agencies and merchant policemen. Representative Samuel Feiwell of South Bend remarked on the bill, "The state had redeemed itself in part. Let us redeem ourselves entirely by repealing this law. Let these men who are so anxious to become policemen file their applications and become officers of the law."[133]

CHAPTER 5

LYNCHING

Lynching has been the predominant method of mobs to carry out vigilante justice. It is a form of punishment that serves as a method of social control to intimidate people. Lynching normally deprives people of their right to due process, and they are punished before their guilt can be proven. The term *lynching* dates back to 1493 in Galway, Ireland. Lynch is one of the most common family names in Ireland. Pierce Lynch served as the first mayor of Galway in 1485; since then, eighty-four mayors have been within the Lynch family lineage. But it was James Fitzstephen Lynch, elected in 1493, who was perhaps the most famous. That year, Lynch's son, Walter, killed a Spanish resident in a moment of jealousy. The public urged that Walter be pardoned. Lynch, who was also a magistrate, believed in justice. He comforted his son in jail before hanging him from a window of their house. Lynch had just become a verb.[134]

From this family sprung Charles Lynch, who immigrated to America in 1725. Upon his death, he bequeathed his large estate to his sons, Charles II and John. In 1786, John received a charter from the Virginia General Assembly establishing a town on their land, present-day Lynchburg, Virginia. But it was the younger Charles whom many people associate with lynching. After Charles was married, he became a Quaker but was soon expelled after enlisting in the Continental army to fight during the American Revolution. Quakers forbade people from taking oaths.[135]

While expelled from the church, Charles held true to the Quaker values. Rising to the rank of colonel, he became responsible for protecting society and supporting the government in the Staunton River region of Virginia.

Charles assembled a band of men to search out Tories, those colonists loyal to the British Crown. Anyone accused or suspected of corresponding with the enemy was brought before Colonel Lynch, who presided as judge. Tories were given due process by confronting their accusers, being permitted to call witnesses and preparing their own defense. If acquitted, they would be released with an apology and reparations. If convicted, punishment would be swift and immediate.[136]

The punishment didn't necessarily mean death, though. Those found guilty were usually flogged, banished from the community or suspended by their thumbs from a walnut tree until they shouted, "Liberty forever!" While lynching has become synonymous with death, there was no instance in which a Tory was sentenced to death. This was attributable to Lynch's Quaker values. His name has become associated with mob law since his death in 1796. However, lynching evolved into an illegal and unjustified execution without due process, unrecognizable during the time of Charles.[137]

According to the Tuskegee Institute, 4,743 people were lynched in the United States from 1882 to 1968. It is almost impossible to know the exact number, which is certainly higher due to the number of unreported lynchings. Of the total number of people lynched during that time period, African Americans accounted for 72 percent, with the majority occurring in the South.[138] The Midwest experienced lynchings, but on a smaller scale. Of the midwestern states, Indiana had the second-lowest number of lynchings among African Americans (18).[139] But that number doesn't include whites, far exceeding the number of Blacks lynched. The reasons for lynching in the South were to intimidate ethnic minorities and enforce white supremacy. In the Midwest, race was not the motivating factor, rather it was to enforce societal rules and what was viewed as a weak court system.

Indiana's criminal justice system lacked two essential elements: certainty and celerity of punishment. Criminals exploited the delays in the administration of justice and took advantage of weak and corrupt judges, sentimental juries and a weak court system to escape punishment. Prosecutors were more concerned with politics than the enforcement of the law. Criminals benefited from highly skilled lawyers who successfully got their clients off. The people had gotten to the point where they feared that justice would never be served unless they took matters into their own hands. Those who favored vigilante justice blamed lawmakers for the increase in lynchings in the state.[140]

However, not everyone supported lynch mobs taking the law into their own hands. After a series of lynchings in Rising Sun in 1839 for larceny, the citizens adopted a resolution condemning the practice. As the first principle of government, order cannot exist without laws, and the people swore to observe and abide by those laws. Lynching puts a public stigma on the entire community.[141] Although the lynchers were tried, the justice system let them off with a $200 fine.[142] In 1887, Governor Isaac Gray said that lynchings were "rapidly bringing the State of Indiana into public disgrace."[143]

The most famous lynching in Indiana occurred in 1868 when ten members of the Reno Gang were killed. The three Reno brothers and Charles Anderson were lynched inside the New Albany Jail after the lynch mob overpowered the sheriff. In 1886, three brothers of the Archer Gang were arrested for murder in Shoals. Like with the Reno brothers, vigilantes took the prisoners from the jail and lynched them before they could be tried. While public opinion was mixed on lynchings, they continued to be used by vigilance committees, White Caps and horse thief detective companies. But a lynching in Versailles in 1898 got the government's attention to try to end the practice.

The Versailles Lynching

For years, the citizens of Versailles in Ripley County were terrorized by a gang of outlaws. After the Civil War, the Levi brothers, Lyle and Isaac, became involved in counterfeiting, having learned the trade from Pete McCartney, one of the nation's most skilled counterfeiters. Their homestead was located in a remote part of the county, allowing them to work in seclusion. Their business became very profitable, with easy access to the Ohio River and nearby counties. In the 1870s, the Levi brothers branched out into horse stealing, going as far as Ohio and Kentucky. A group of farmers formed a vigilante group to stop the thefts occurring in Ripley County.[144]

The Levi brothers' sister, Missouri, married James Rittenhouse, and they owned about forty acres of land in nearby Osgood. He became a gang member by marriage and soon became the group leader. The Levi brothers taught him how to counterfeit money, and his work soon surpassed that of his teachers. He discovered a method of imitating gold that baffled even Secret Service agents. They eventually formed an alliance with the Driggs Gang in Dayton, Ohio. Rittenhouse was eventually arrested and sentenced to fourteen years in the Jeffersonville Prison, while Missouri, affectionately called the "Queen of the Counterfeiters," was sent to the women's reformatory in Indianapolis. Missouri convinced a federal judge to release her husband, as he was ill. This was a ruse, and Rittenhouse fled to Mexico after being released. Missouri returned to her home in Osgood with her two brothers, who also served time for counterfeiting.[145]

The gang began to grow, and various crimes were perpetrated against the citizens of Ripley County. They would burglarize by night and rob by day. Farmers would bring their cattle into town to be sold, and the next day, the cows would all be dead or wounded on the side of the road. They would torture men and women. Elderly German women would be forced to stand on a hot stove until they revealed the location of some supposedly hidden treasure in the house. Although they were arrested at times, they were able to cover up their crimes, and they were rarely convicted.[146]

Versailles had a population of eight hundred people, but it was five miles from any railroad station and had no telegraphic communication with the outside world. As the county seat of Ripley County, it was literally cut off from the rest of the state. There was an increase in robberies in all parts of the county. Ripley County sheriff Henry Bushing received a tip from an informant that the gang was planning to rob the Wooley Brothers store in Correct, ten miles from Versailles. The sheriff deputized five men and went to Correct to lay in wait. The sheriff positioned himself in the cellar, while the deputies took up positions around the building.[147]

Shortly after midnight, three gang members—Clifford Gordon, Bert Andrews and the sheriff's informant—broke into the business. The sheriff immediately seized Gordon by the arm. Gordon and the sheriff both pulled out revolvers and began firing. The deputies came to the sheriff's rescue. More than thirty shots were fired. The sheriff was shot in the hand, and Gordon was shot several times but managed to escape with Andrews and the informant. Andrews and Gordon were later arrested in Osgood. The horse buggy they were using belonged to Lyle Levi, and the robbery was planned at the home of William Jenkins. They were arrested as accessories. A fifth person, Henry Schulter, was arrested for robbing the barbershop in Osgood. They were all taken to the jail in Versailles.[148]

When it became known that they were in jail, a group of concerned citizens suggested that "justice" be administered. Around 1:00 a.m. on Wednesday, September 15, 1897, a group of men on horseback, numbering four hundred, dismounted in Versailles. While the sheriff was at home recovering from his injuries, the jail was left in the hands of the sheriff's brother-in-law, William Kenan. He and four other deputies were on duty in the jail residence that night. There was a knock on the door at 2:00 a.m., and three masked men with revolvers greeted Kenan. Kenan was forced to hand over the keys, and the mob filed into the jail. Levi, Jenkins and Schulter were on the ground floor, while Gordon and Andrews were upstairs.[149]

Some of the members did not go with the mob quietly. Schulter was shot in the chest, and Jenkins and Andrews were struck over the head with a stool. A noose was placed around each of the five prisoners' necks, and they were dragged about two hundred yards to an elm tree. Levi, Jenkins and Schulter were already dead, but they were hanged anyway. Gordon and Andrews met their death by hanging. The bodies remained hanging as the sun rose and were brought down after Justice of the Peace Charles Loswell held an inquest.[150]

The citizens were unfazed by the lynching, and there was talk of lynching more gang members. There was a rumor that Andrews was innocent of the crime. He had sent a note to Marshal Dan Gilliland in Osgood detailing the plans of the burglary. Andrews did not attempt to shoot anyone, and he only ran after being shot at by the deputies. The note was not discovered until after the lynching. It is unknown if Andrews knew that the other gang member was acting as an informant for the sheriff.[151]

Upon hearing the news of the lynching, Governor Mount sent Assistant Attorney General Merrill Moore to investigate. He was met with resistance, as people refused to talk. Governor Mount gave a statement regarding the lynching:

> *I think the lax enforcement of the law has brought about this disgraceful act at the hands of lynchers in Ripley County. I understand the thieving and systematic robbery have been carried on there and that the criminals have not been promptly brought to justice. While this failure to enforce law may have occurred, yet it is no justification for mob law. No matter what the pretext is, men who take the enforcement of law into their own hands and lynch men shall be punished in Indiana. It makes no difference what crime these outlaws have committed, they are entitled to an impartial trial before punishment. When men are denied the right to a fair trial at the hands of a competent court, we are in the midst of revolution and anarchy, and that condition shall not exist in Indiana.*[152]

The investigation was met with further resistance. The citizens refused to assist in bringing the lynchers to justice, and local lawyers refused to help the prosecutors. A detective from Indianapolis was shot and killed while investigating the lynching. After that, no detective would take the case, and Governor Mount was forced to contact the Secret Service for help. Detective

William Burns, a highly successful agent, initially hesitated to take the case because it had nothing to do with counterfeiting. At the urging of the chief of the Secret Service, Burns accepted the assignment. He spent four months undercover, posing as an insurance agent.[153]

Only one person, Hezekiah Hughes, was ever indicted for the lynchings, accused of shooting Schulter. The trial was held in Cross Plains. Attorney General William Ketchum prosecuted the case for the state. Not one witness cooperated with the prosecution, claiming that they did not witness or know anything about the lynchings. The judge, a friend of Hughes, ruled that the evidence was insufficient to convict him. Instead, he gave perhaps the most absurd explanation ever given when he said that the evidence showed that the five men broke out of jail and committed suicide—even as the coroner's inquest ruled their death homicide at the hands of a lynch mob. Governor Mount and Ketchum had to accept defeat and realized that no one would ever be held accountable.[154]

Nine months later, another lynching in nearby Scott County again rocked the state. On December 24, a mob lynched Marion Tyler for the attempted murder of his wife, Laura. After the couple was married, they moved from Scottsburg to Indianapolis. Laura filed for divorce and moved back home. On November 3, Marion went to Scottsburg to reconcile with his wife. After things did not go his way, Marion pulled a revolver, shot his wife in the head and fired a second round in her side while she lay on the ground. The wounds were not fatal, and she got up and ran from him. Marion then tried to commit suicide by shooting himself in the head. After that failed to kill him, he shot himself a second time in the abdomen. Marion eventually recovered from his wounds and was charged with attempted murder.[155]

For nearly three weeks, he was held in the county jail under the supervision of a nurse during the day and guards at night. There were rumors throughout the town of lynching him. It was not known why the lynch mob targeted Marion. He was mostly a stranger without money or friends to help him escape justice. It was believed that he had evidence against some people in town that could be damaging.[156] A group of thirty masked men accosted Sheriff Gobin, who gave the bandits the keys and a lamp and told them where they could find Marion Tyler. The mob took Tyler outside and hanged him from a tree before fleeing into the night. Many felt that Sheriff Gobin willingly helped the bandits. The coroner said that Tyler's life could have been saved, but instead of cutting Tyler down, Sheriff Gobin went around town for thirty minutes telling everyone what had happened. The coroner believed that it took nearly twenty minutes for Tyler to die.[157]

ANTI-LYNCHING LEGISLATION

In the wake of the two lynchings, Governor Mount looked at passing anti-lynching legislation to deter vigilante mobs from taking the law into their own hands. He drew inspiration from Ohio, which passed an anti-lynching law in 1896 that made the county liable for damages for lynchings within its borders. Mount's bill would give the widow and children of lynching victims the right to sue the county for damages up to $5,000. The sheriff could be ousted from office if someone was lynched in his custody. The bill would also allow the trial to be moved to another county. Under Indiana law, the person had the right to be tried in the county where the crime occurred. In the Hughes trial in Versailles, which was a farce, the trial was opened with a prayer by a church pastor, from whose congregation the accused and the judge were both members. Getting a fair trial in the county where a lynching took place was almost impossible.[158]

Mount's anti-lynching legislation met resistance when it was defeated in the House by a vote of 35 to 60. Those opposing the bill were concerned that innocent taxpayers would have to foot the bill and that the families of criminals would be rewarded. Supporters of the bill were frustrated that they were more concerned with money instead with trying to prevent mob rule and unjustified murder.[159] While the legislature continued to argue the particulars of the anti-lynching bill, John Tyler, the father of Marion, refused to wait on Indiana and filed a civil suit against Sheriff Gobin for negligence. Since there was no anti-lynching bill in Indiana and he lived in Illinois, the case was filed in federal court in Indianapolis. He was seeking $5,000 in damages. Tyler won the case, but it came at a cost. The jury awarded $5 in damages, and the court costs, which were $1,000, were the plaintiff's responsibility. The verdict was baffling, as the court showed that human life is only worth $5. This was the first such case that was brought in Indiana.[160]

While the Tyler case was being heard in federal court, the legislature finally agreed on an anti-lynching bill. The new law included the original provisions first submitted by Governor Mount. It also defined "mob" as a collection of individuals assembled for any unlawful purpose intending to injure any person by violence and without the authority of law. Any act of violence exercised by a mob would constitute the crime of lynching. Anyone who participates or aids and abets shall receive the death penalty or life imprisonment.[161] Citizens are required to assist the sheriff, when requested, in protecting the prisoner or defending against the mob. Refusal to assist could result in imprisonment from one to two years.[162]

The law was challenged in 1900 when an angry mob lynched three Black residents in Rockport, in Spencer County. On December 17, Joseph Rolla, Bud Rowland and Jim Henderson were arrested for the murder of Hollie Simons, a white barber. Simons had been brutally beaten and robbed earlier that morning. Thousands of people took to the streets looking for the killers. Rowland and Henderson were arrested later that afternoon as suspects. A bloodhound from Kentucky led the mob to the home of Rowland, confirming to the mob that he was guilty.

With no attempt to disguise themselves, the enraged mob used a sledgehammer to break into the jail. The officers did not put up a fight. Rowland and Henderson were dragged to the courthouse lawn by a rope around their necks. After fully confessing to the murder, they were hanged in front of a crowd of thousands. The crowd then fired hundreds of rounds into the bodies as they hung. Shortly before their death, they implicated a third person in the murder, Joseph Rolla. Sheriff Oatley Anderson arrested Rolla the next day, as he had already confessed that he struck the first blow against Simons.[163]

Sheriff Anderson, fearing that another lynching was possible, decided to move Rolla to Boonville in neighboring Warrick County. The secret didn't take long to get out, and the mob headed for Boonville. The mob numbered over two hundred men. Warrick County sheriff Benjamin Hudson was out of town, so the jail was under the control of Deputy Sheriff Raymond Cherry. He refused to give the mob the keys. Still, they successfully used a battering ram to bust a hole through the building. They took Rolla and hanged him from a tree outside the jail. As soon as the mob had dispersed, a company of National Guard soldiers from Evansville showed up, having been ordered out by the governor.[164]

Governor Mount was partly blamed for the lynching of Rolla. He had already been notified that a second lynching was possible. After being assured by Sheriff Anderson that he would be able to protect Rolla, Governor Mount appeared to be satisfied. However, the sheriff proved that he couldn't protect Henderson or Rowland, so it wasn't likely that he could protect Rolla. The public felt that the governor should have immediately dispatched the militia to take custody of Rolla. Instead, the militia arrived a little too late.[165]

Two weeks after the lynching in Spencer County, Indiana had a new governor, Winfield Durbin. The legislature strengthened the anti-lynching law. If a prisoner in the sheriff's custody was lynched, it would be conclusive evidence of a neglect of duty, and the office would be immediately vacated. The county coroner would take over as sheriff until the next election. The sheriff would also be ineligible for reappointment or reelection. The governor would have the sole power to reinstate the sheriff only upon petition within ten days and satisfactory evidence that he used all of the powers of his office to protect the prisoner. The law basically vacated the office of the sheriff at the exact moment that a lynching occurs.[166]

CASE OF SHERIFF JOHN DUDLEY

The first case under the new law occurred on November 22, 1902, in Sullivan County. James Dillard, a Black man, had assaulted two women in Sullivan, Indiana. He fled to Lawrenceville, Illinois, where he was shot three times by the city marshal after he attempted to arrest him.[167] Sullivan County sheriff John Dudley went to Illinois and took custody of the wounded Dillard. The State of Illinois considered filing kidnapping charges against Dudley for taking Dillard without completing the extradition process.[168]

After a lynch mob took Dillard from the jail and hanged him, under the new law, Sheriff Dudley automatically forfeited his office. The county coroner, William P. Maxwell, took over the sheriff's office. Sheriff Dudley petitioned the governor to be reinstated, but Governor Durbin refused. Sheriff Dudley filed a lawsuit, and the court found the anti-lynching law unconstitutional. The court held that the legislature could not declare any fact conclusive evidence that a person is guilty. Every person was entitled to due process. The Indiana Supreme Court confirmed it, and Dudley was reinstated as sheriff.[169] In 1905, the law was amended so that a sheriff can only be removed through a criminal proceeding initiated by the attorney general.[170]

The law dramatically decreased lynchings and mob violence, as sheriffs were determined to save their jobs by increasing security at their jails. While Governor Durbin successfully curbed vigilante justice, the murder rate during his administration dramatically increased. Many blamed the increase in murders on the anti-lynching laws, as criminals no longer feared mob violence, as well as the lax enforcement of the laws. In Allen County, a man stabbed his wife's brother, but since he didn't die, he was released with a twenty-five-dollar fine.[171] In 1904, the last year of Durbin's administration, there were six murder trials tried simultaneously. Only one of those ended in a conviction, and it was for a lesser offense of second-degree murder.[172] At the same time, politicians were asking for the death penalty to be abolished. The argument was that the death penalty did not deter crime and was nothing more than legalized murder. If it wasn't okay for individuals to murder people, the same was true for the government.[173] The issue had become that criminals no longer feared the law.

After the Sullivan County lynching, the practice was abolished for nearly thirty years, until August 7, 1930, in Marion, Indiana. Two young African Americans, Thomas Shipp and Abram Smith, were lynched by a mob of thousands after being accused of robbery, murder and rape. They were taken from their cells, beaten and hanged from a tree in the courthouse square. The mob took pieces of their clothing as souvenirs. A third suspect, sixteen-year-old James Cameron, narrowly escaped death at the hands of the mob. This was the last known lynching in Indiana. Lynching was finally designated as a hate crime on March 29, 2022, when President Joe Biden signed the Emmett Till Antilynching Act, named for a Chicago teenager killed in Mississippi in 1955.[174]

Lynching is a dark stain on the country's history, regardless of whether it is used to intimidate Black Americans or enforce vigilante justice. There are undoubtedly issues with the criminal justice system, and the outcome may not always be fair, but everyone is still entitled to due process. Lynching has no place in society. As it was stated in the past and still holds true today, "Lynching is a crime against law and society, and no man has a right to call himself a law-abiding citizen who engages in it."[175]

CHAPTER 6

AMERICAN PROTECTIVE LEAGUE

While most Americans supported the U.S. entry into World War I, a minority of people bitterly opposed it. Before entering the war, the United States was experiencing major labor unrest that often erupted into bloody conflicts. Extremist groups promoted the doctrine of workers' control over production and encouraged violence. One such group was the Industrial Workers of the World (IWW), whose philosophy is described as "revolutionary industrial unionism"; the group also has ties to socialist and anarchist labor movements.[176] The IWW was vehemently opposed to the war.

Along with anarchist labor groups, the Wilson administration also had to contend with pro-German sympathizers who had joined ranks with the American Socialist Party to protest the war. On July 30, 1916, a munitions warehouse on Black Tom Island in New York Harbor exploded, the result of sabotage. Before the United States entered the war, the warehouse supplied munitions to the Allies fighting in Europe. German agents attempted to disrupt this by attacking the munitions depot. The explosion resulted in four deaths and more than one hundred injured, resulting in $25 million ($500 million in 2023) in damages. The explosion even damaged a portion of the Statue of Liberty.[177] This event helped change America's public opinion of Germany and pushed the United States closer to war.

President Woodrow Wilson maintained that the United States would remain neutral at the start of World War I, which most Americans favored. That position of neutrality was challenged in 1915 when the British vessel

Lusitania was sunk by a German U-boat, claiming the lives of almost 2,000 passengers, including 128 Americans. After the Zimmerman telegram was intercepted, suggesting an alliance between Mexico and Germany, President Wilson asked Congress to declare war against Germany. The United States officially entered World War I on April 6, 1917.

As the nation entered the war, America's civil liberties also became threatened. President Wilson created the Committee on Public Information to mobilize support for the war. The committee launched a campaign to sell the war by utilizing writers, actors and scholars to give speeches nationwide. Those who opposed the war were labeled as traitors. Immigrants were forced to abandon their native cultures for "Americanization." Libraries began to burn German books, communities banned German music and German was eliminated from school curriculums. There was a renaming of anything Germanic, as sauerkraut became "liberty cabbage" and German measles became "liberty measles." Some people were even forced to change their last name for fear of being beaten or lynched.[178] In Indiana, East Germantown in Wayne County was renamed Pershing after General John Pershing, commander of American forces in World War I.[179]

When the United States entered the war, the U.S. Army ranked seventh in the world in terms of size. America had 200,000 enlisted soldiers compared to 4.5 million in Germany. To mobilize a fighting force, Congress passed the Selective Service Act in 1917, which required all men, ages twenty-one to thirty, to register for the draft. In 1918, the age range was changed to eighteen to forty-five. More than 10 million people registered on the first day, and by the war's end, it had risen to 22 million. While many young men answered the call to serve, there were about 350,000 people who refused to register. Organizations like the IWW actively encouraged draft resistance.[180]

To crack down on dissent, Congress passed the Espionage Act in 1917. It prohibited interference with the draft and outlawed criticism of the government or the war effort. Any activities considered disloyal, false statements intended to interfere with military operations or false statements promoting the success of America's enemies were forbidden. The U.S. Post Office was authorized to intercept any mail deemed seditious, anarchistic or treasonous. The act made violations committed during wartime punishable by death.[181] Congress attempted to include the censorship of newspapers as part of the act, but after a national protest, it was removed.[182] This just illustrated the enormous lengths the government tried to stifle dissent in the United States.

The Bureau of Investigation (BOI) only had 219 field agents in the United States and was overwhelmed trying to enforce the Espionage Act. A wealthy Chicago advertising executive, Albert Briggs, proposed a voluntary civilian organization to help supplement the federal government. It received approval from Attorney General Thomas Gregory and President Wilson. This new organization, designated "the powerful right arm of America's secret service," would be called the American Protective League (APL).

The APL soon had more than 250,000 members in major cities and small towns throughout the United States. Members included bank presidents, railroad heads, judges, lawyers and titans of industry. But the organization also included office workers and homemakers. No one was overlooked. There was only one qualification: "red-blooded Americansim and 100 percent patriotic."

Although it was a private organization, it was given legitimacy by the federal government. They wore badges and had a quasi-official status: "American Protective League—Secret Service." Although the League operated under the Department of Justice, the Secret Service voiced concerns that its title implied that they worked for the Treasury Department. The national headquarters was in Washington, D.C., with field offices throughout the country.[183]

Members conducted surveillance and went on raids of German immigrants, German sympathizers and draft dodgers. Americans who attempted to resist the draft were known as "slackers," and APL members would go on raids, rounding up those who resisted the draft law.[184] They specifically targeted the IWW, and at rallies and protests, members would make people sign a loyalty card.[185] Members would go after those who violated the war regulations on food and gasoline. The national office began to lose control over its members. They used their status to make illegal arrests. In New York City, members arrested more than fifty thousand people over a ten-day period, which garnered the attention of Congress. Attorney General Gregory was forced to announce that APL members would not be used to arrest civilians.[186]

By the time the United States entered World War I, Indiana had the twelfth-largest German population in the country.[187] Germans formed the largest percentage of foreigners in Indiana. Some counties, such as Dubois and Wayne, had large German populations, while major cities like Evansville, Indianapolis and Fort Wayne were also a draw. Indiana's German population grew so much that an 1869 law was passed mandating that schools teach German as a branch of study as long as twenty-five students requested it. While most German immigrants were farmers, the new law opened up different career opportunities. Although students were not obligated to learn German, half of the school population took advantage of the opportunity.[188] German was a required subject in school until 1910, when it became an elective.

When public opinion turned against Germany, it also turned against German residents who had lived in the United States for decades. Many of those German residents were not U.S. citizens. Under the Indiana Constitution, foreigners could vote as long as they declared their intention to become naturalized citizens. Many of them never followed through with completing the process of becoming full U.S. citizens. When the war broke out, the federal government classified German and Austrian residents as "enemy aliens." This new class prevented them from living or working in restricted zones, including military installations, industrial areas and government buildings. To enter a restricted zone required a permit issued by the state's U.S. marshal.[189]

An unusual dilemma arose in Michigan City, which had a considerable German population. The federal government had restricted major city areas as off limits to Germans, including the city center, harbors and a vehicle manufacturing facility with a government contract. More than six hundred Germans in Michigan City were enemy aliens who required a permit. This included a police sergeant who couldn't go to the police station and two city council members unable to attend council meetings without one. The federal government had suspended the naturalization process until the war was over, keeping thousands of Germans in limbo.[190]

Ironically, Michigan City's mayor, Martin Kruger, was considered one of the best-known Germans in the state. He had unsuccessfully run for Congress multiple times.[191] In 1917, the mayoral race was between Republican Samuel Taylor and Democrat Fred C. Miller. Miller had previously been the mayor of Michigan City for two terms before losing a third bid to Kruger in 1913. Although Miller was victorious at the polls, the election was contested, resulting in three people claiming the office.

Not wanting to relinquish the office to Miller, Mayor Kruger filed a federal lawsuit claiming that Miller was an enemy alien and, therefore, could not be mayor. Taylor claimed that the office belonged to him because Miller was ineligible. Kruger argued that Taylor had no claim to the office because he lost. Kruger was attempting to stay in office indefinitely. Michigan City had three mayors working out of different parts of the city for a short time.

After President Wilson refused to intervene and the federal lawsuit was dismissed for lack of jurisdiction, the case was filed in Superior Court in LaPorte County.[192] The case was then transferred to Valparaiso, where it was ruled that Miller was the rightful mayor of Michigan City.[193] As the mayor, he was still required to obtain a permit to occupy city hall. Senators Harry New and James Watson had argued against Miller becoming the mayor. In the wake of the court decision, they urged that the laws be changed to prevent unnaturalized citizens from holding elective office.[194]

Civil liberties were further threatened with the passage of the Sedition Act in 1918. It forbade the uttering or printing of anything deemed "disloyal, profane, scurrilous, or abusive" language about the U.S. government, the military or the flag. It also penalized those who spoke favorably of Germany or its allies. The postmaster general could refuse to deliver mail that contained such language. Speech became punishable by up to twenty years imprisonment and a $10,000 fine.[195] Indiana native Eugene Debs, one of the founders of the IWW and five-time Socialist Party presidential candidate, was arrested for a speech he gave in Canton, Ohio. He urged Americans to resist the draft and was later charged with ten counts of sedition. He was sentenced to ten years in prison.[196]

To finance the war, the government sold liberty bonds. The Sedition Act also penalized anyone who attempted to interfere with the sale of those bonds. The APL went after individuals who did not buy bonds. A storekeeper in Michigan City was given an ultimatum to either buy bonds or get out of town. He ended up buying $400 in liberty bonds. A pastor in South Bend was expelled from the Minister's Association because of his pro-German sentiments and his refusal to support the liberty bonds.[197]

The APL contributed to a sense of paranoia spreading throughout the country. People became suspicious of their neighbors and sometimes family members. People were afraid to speak ill of the government or the war, even in their own homes, for fear of being discovered and reported to the APL. Young boys were even recruited to seek out the "yellow dog," someone who praised or aided Germany. A yellow dog could be someone who whines about the war or claims that it is a rich man's war, who complains about the draft or the impossibility of defeating Germany. The suppression of yellow dogs was of utmost concern. Young boys were recruited from the Boy Scouts and the YMCA into a new organization called the Boy Detectives of America. The boys were given membership cards. They were also given yellow dog cards, and whenever a boy heard someone complaining or talking bad about the government, they would hand the card to them to be put on notice.[198]

World War I officially ended on November 11, 1918. With Germany defeated, the APL officially disbanded on February 1, 1919. It was estimated that the organization carried out more than 3 million investigations.[199] The federal government commended them for their unselfish duty to protect their country. After the war ended, Indiana continued its persecution of the German people. In February 1919, Indiana was one of thirty-four states that banned the teaching of German in public schools.[200] German was no longer spoken outside the home, students burned German books and the German-language newspaper *Telegraph und Tribune* ceased publication. Even dachshunds came under scrutiny. It had fallen out of the top ten dog breeds in the United States, and small boys would unleash bulldogs and terriers on the German breed.[201]

The APL was unique among vigilante groups because of its federal government support. At a time when vigilante groups were mostly local or regional, the federal government, for the first time, had nationalized vigilantism.

GALLERY 1

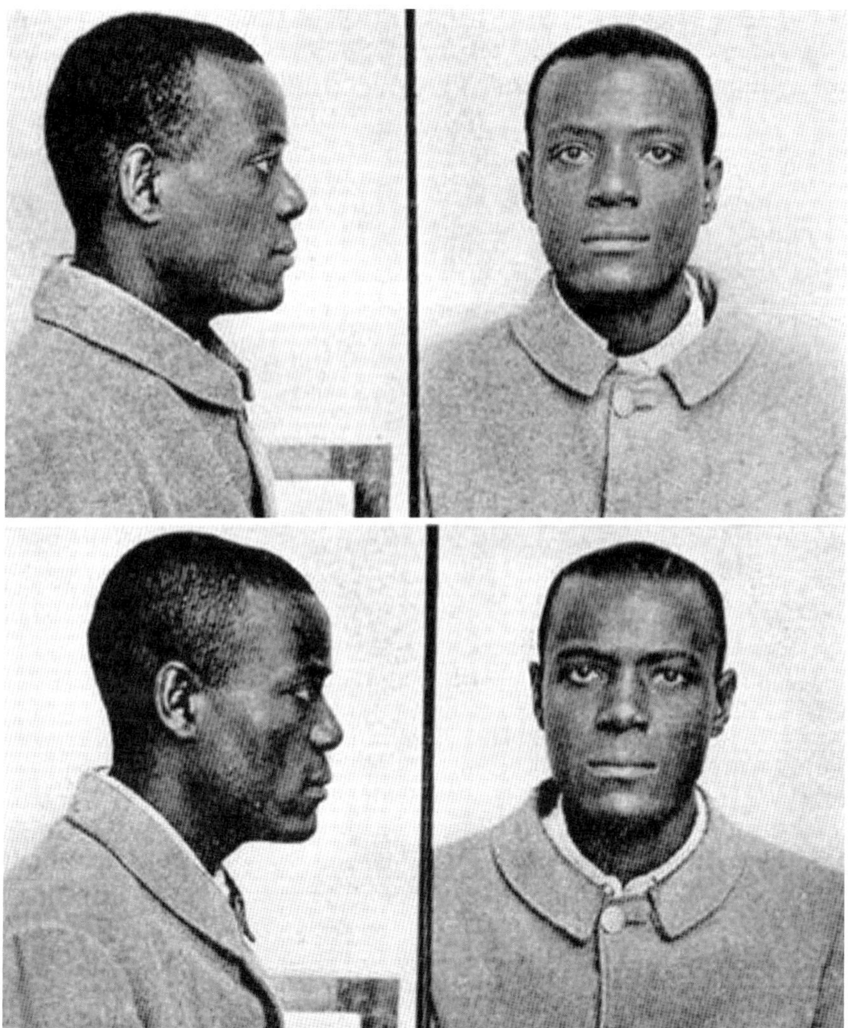

The case of William and Will West showed the flaws in the Bertillion system and how fingerprints were a superior method of identification. *Public domain image.*

FRANKLIN

National Horse Thieves Detective Association Oct. 4. 1904.

Opposite: Group photos of an Indiana Horse Thief Detective company. *National Horse Thief Detective Association Collection, Robert T. Ramsay Jr. Archival Center, Lilly Library, Wabash College, Crawfordsville, Indiana.*

Above, left: George Barrett, the first person to be executed by hanging under a new law making it a capital offense to kill a federal agent. *From* The Times, *March 24, 1936.*

Above, right: Patrolman John J. Gerka Jr. *From* The Times, *May 15, 1941.*

Right: Fred C. Miller, mayor of Michigan City, who had won reelection in 1917. His election was challenged in court as an alleged enemy alien for being German. *From* The Times, *November 25, 1938.*

Above: Advertisement for Liberty Bonds, which were used to help finance World War I. *Library of Congress*.

Opposite, top left: Lillian Holley, sheriff of Lake County, Indiana, when John Dillinger broke out of the jail. *From the* Sumter Daily Item, *March 6, 1934*.

Opposite, top right: Eugene Teague, shot and killed by the Dillinger Gang, was the first Indiana State Police officer killed in the line of duty. *Indiana State Police Museum*.

Opposite, bottom: The different badges worn by more than three thousand people in Marion County with arrest powers. *From the* Indianapolis Times, *September 21, 1925*.

SOME OF THE '15 VARIETIES'

Horse Thief Detective | Police | Constable | State Motorpolice

Federal Prohibition Agent | United States Marshal | Private Detective | Fish and Game Warden.

Above are eight of the fifteen kin ds of badges a Times survey showed are worn in Marion County by the 3,350 persons empowered to make arrests and carry guns.

2,000 U. S. REFUGEES REACH NATIVE SHORES

French ahd Itallan Steamers Put In to New York Harbor With Americans From Havre and Naples.

NEW YORK, Aug. 20.—Two more ship loads of Americans who were in Europe when war began, returned home by way of this port today. The French liner France brought nearly 1,400 from Havre and the Stampalia of LaVeloce lines, 633 from Italy.

Of two outgoing transatlantic steam-

An Active Figure in Food Probe Here.

A. F. KEARNEY.

Top: Individuals involved in the Clinton bank robbery. *Top, from left to right*: Thomas Bell, G.W. Landis and Walter Dietrich. *Bottom, from left to right*: E.E. Boetta, Patrolman Walter Burnside and Police Chief Everett Helms. *From the* Indianapolis Star, *December 18, 1930.*

Bottom: A.F. Kearney, the first agent in charge of the FBI's Indianapolis field office. *From the* Indianapolis Star, *August 21, 1914.*

J. Edgar Hoover, first director of the FBI, 1935–72. *Library of Congress.*

Lynching of Bud Rowland and Jim Henderson. *From the* Indianapolis News, *December 18, 1900.*

Indiana Motor Vehicle Police, October 23, 1923. *Indiana State Police Museum.*

POSSES LEAVE IN PURSUIT OF DILLINGER

Civilian posse organizes to go after John Dillinger. *From the* Indianapolis News, *March 5, 1934.*

Right: Felix Stidger, Union spy who infiltrated the Knights of the Golden Circle. *From the* Indianapolis News, *May 15, 1908.*

Below: The five conspirators of the Knights of the Golden Circle tried for conspiring to assassinate Governor Morton. *From the* Indianapolis Journal, *September 4, 1892.*

Opposite, top: Cryptic messages used by the Knights of the Golden Circle to communicate with one another. *From the* Daily Republican, *August 5, 1908.*

Opposite, middle: Advertisement for Liberty Bonds, used during World War I. *Library of Congress.*

Opposite, bottom: Five men of the Reno Gang were lynched in 1897 at the Ripley County Jail in Versailles. *From the* Bedford Daily Times, *December 12, 1971.*

FELIX GRUNDY STIDGER.

FIVE OF THE CONSPIRATORS.

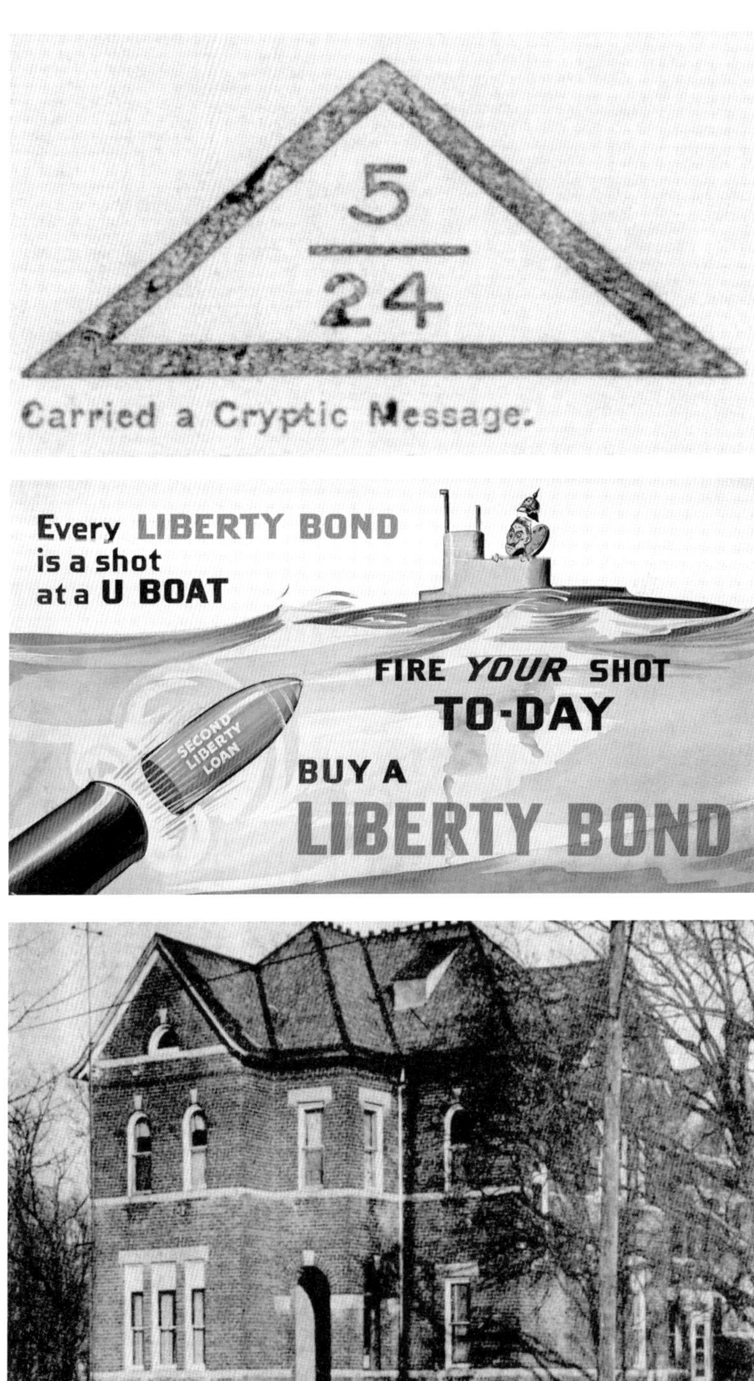
5
24
Carried a Cryptic Message.
Every LIBERTY BOND
is a shot
at a U BOAT
FIRE YOUR SHOT
TO-DAY
SECOND LIBERTY LOAN
BUY A
LIBERTY BOND

Top, left: Manson Burrell, the first and only agent killed in the line of duty in Indiana from the Federal Narcotics Bureau (predecessor to the DEA). *Public domain image.*

Top, right: A sign recognizing the origin of the Lynch Law in America. The sign is located in Altavista in Campbell County, Virginia. *From the* News and Advance, *July 31, 2005.*

Bottom: Two Indianapolis police rapid trucks, purchased in 1909. *Patrick Pearsey.*

CHAPTER 7

BANKING VIGILANTES

From its founding, Tolleston, Indiana, primarily consisted of German immigrants and railroad workers. Tolleston had become an independent city in 1906 to prevent annexation by Gary, which was also founded that same year. After Gary got into a dispute with East Chicago in 1910, Tolleston became a casualty and was annexed by Gary. The State Bank of Tolleston survived to carry on the name.

On July 14, 1919, five armed bandits entered the State Bank of Tolleston, where a dozen people were crowded in the lobby. One of the bandits gave the command, "Throw up your hands." The cashier, C.E. Phillips, and the bank president, Herman Uecker, were behind the counter. As the patrons did as instructed, Uecker reached for a revolver and was instantly shot by the bandits. Five shots were fired, and Uecker received two of them and was pronounced dead on the scene. Phillips took one round to the leg. The suspects fled the bank empty-handed and escaped in a stolen Hudson Super-Six.[202]

The bank issued a $5,000 reward for the apprehension of the suspects. In a classic case of a woman scorned, one of the suspect's wives revealed their identities to the Chicago police. She was in the process of trying to divorce her husband, Albert Batchelor, and believed that if she could get him arrested, it would be easier for her to get a divorce.[203] After she supplied the police with his identity, the authorities identified his accomplices.

Albert Batchelor was part of a violent gang responsible for several robberies in Chicago and Gary. They were suspected of shooting a police officer during a gas station robbery. When they were not committing armed robberies, they were stealing motor vehicles. Brothers Dan and Nick Trkulja ran a taxi business in Gary. Nick was regarded as one of the biggest auto thieves in the country,[204] and his garage doubled as a chop shop. The stolen vehicle used in the robbery came from his garage. Dan was considered to be the leader of the gang. He supplied the guns and formulated the plan.[205] Thomas Batchelor, Albert's brother, was the only one of the group who was married with a family, and they lived in Valparaiso, while James Harry (Red) Parker was from Chicago. Two others, Lee Spiers and Damjan Bielich, were accessories and assisted with their escape.

This was the fourth robbery of the bank within the last five years. Understandably, there was public outrage at the senseless, cold-blooded murder. But what angered the residents more than anything was the failure of the parole system. All of the suspects except for the Trkulja brothers were on parole. There was a fear that the government was turning prisoners loose, and that would affect the safety of the public.[206]

The four bandits—the Batchelor brothers, Dan Trkulja and Harry Parker—all confessed and pleaded guilty. Within twenty-four hours of their plea, Judge Martin Smith of Lake County sentenced all four suspects to die by electrocution no later than November 1, a mere five months away.[207] Lee Spiers and Danjan Bielich were sentenced to life in prison. Nick Trkulja was found guilty of manslaughter for his role as an accessory before and after the fact. His life was threatened to such an extent that the sheriff had to transfer him to the state prison for fear of the mob exacting vigilante justice.[208]

While many applauded the death sentence, state senator Franklin McCray, who was also an attorney, intervened on their behalf. Senator McCray believed that only a jury could hand down a death sentence, especially when they pleaded guilty.[209] The Indiana Supreme Court ruled in favor of the four men and ordered a new trial. The trial was moved to Valparaiso, and all four men had their death sentences commuted to life in prison.[210] Batchelor's wife, who was responsible for their capture, was denied the reward money, and it was divided up between the Gary and Chicago Police Departments.

Indiana residents, especially those in rural areas, had cause to be alarmed after the Tolleston State Bank robbery. Banks were popping up all over the state in small rural towns. The Tolleston State Bank was situated in a heavily populated area, and if bandits could easily rob the bank, a single town constable was no match. Gangs of criminals had systematically taken advantage of the unprotected rural banks, post offices and stores. They were using stolen automobiles, most of which were faster than anything the police were using. A crime wave had overtaken the state, and rural residents were begging for help.[211]

The sheriff-constable plan was ineffective during emergencies. Bank robberies happened more frequently, and law enforcement could not keep up. The people were outraged at the government, and the government was humiliated for not being able to keep their residents safe.[212] As a means to protect the state's rural areas, state senator Arthur Baxter proposed a bill creating a state police force. He pointed to the efficiency of other states that had made one, and it was pushing bandits into states like Indiana, which were unprotected.[213] What they got was a motor vehicle unit consisting of seventeen officers responsible for the whole state. It was more of a slap in the face to the rural residents who were left to their own devices.

BANK ROBBERY ON THE RISE

After World War I, the U.S. economy became the largest in the world, while Europe dealt with the financial fallout from the war. The economic center of the world moved from London to Wall Street. After the Panic of 1907, the Federal Reserve Act of 1913 was enacted to stabilize the U.S. banking system. It also allowed state banks to be regulated by the Federal Reserve. By 1915, there were 18,227 state banks along with 7,598 national banks throughout the United States.[214] In Indiana, 1,008 banks in 1916 steadily increased to 1,108 banks in 1924. There was very little regulation, and most of these banks were located in rural areas, which made them a prime target for criminals.[215]

Beginning in 1920, Prohibition began with the passage of the Eighteenth Amendment. This led to increased organized crime and spurred a national crime wave. Bank robberies, kidnappings, auto theft and gambling had become commonplace, and the rural areas were heavily targeted. Law enforcement could not keep up, and jurisdictional issues further hobbled them. The authorities did not want to pursue criminals beyond their borders. The Bureau of Investigation (BOI) was still fairly young, understaffed and had a reputation for politicized investigations.[216]

Indiana was not the only state dealing with the rise in crime. Iowa experienced 106 bank robberies, with a total loss of $489,888 between the years 1919 and 1921.[217] Illinois experienced 88 bank robberies, with a total loss of $590,000 in just over a year between 1924 and 1925. During that same time, Indiana experienced 33 bank robberies, with a loss of $88,000.[218]

THE EDWARDSPORT STATE BANK ROBBERY

Edwardsport is a small town in Knox County, the oldest county in Indiana. During the 1920s, it was still pretty much a rural county, with its largest city being Vincennes. There were a lot of mine workers in and around Edwardsport. The Edwardsport State Bank was busy, especially on payday, when the miners would show up to cash their paychecks. Due to its rural location, it was robbed in the summer of 1923 of $3,000. The bandits were eventually caught and sentenced to prison for ten to twenty years.[219] In nearby Spencer, in Owen County, thieves robbed two banks around the same time and made off with $17,000.[220]

On November 8, 1923, it was payday for the miners. Two miners, William Jones and Theodore Armstrong, never showed up to work. Instead, they conned a farmer out of a jug of moonshine. After consuming the alcohol, they entered the Edwardsport State Bank around noon. The business district was deserted, and the cashier, Charles Wright, was the only one in the bank. Realizing that it was payday and there would be a lot of money on hand, they held it up. Wright was in the process of starting a fire when the bandits entered the bank. As he stood up, Armstrong, perhaps a bit too inebriated, reacted rashly and shot Wright twice, with fatal results. The suspects fled the scene in a vehicle. They were identified as they fired shots at farmers as they sped out of town.[221]

There was so much outrage over the senseless murder that a mob of citizens had gathered around the jail. Fearing that the mob would take justice into their own hands, the two suspects were taken to an undisclosed location for their safety.[222] Theodore Armstrong would later plead guilty and was sentenced to life in prison.[223] William Jones confessed to the crime but later recanted his testimony. He pleaded not guilty and had his trial moved to Bloomfield in neighboring Greene County. A jury found him guilty of first-degree murder and sentenced him to life in prison.[224]

THE BANK VIGILANTE MOVEMENT BEGINS

During the preceding six years, daytime bank robberies were uncommon. Nighttime bank burglaries were the norm. However, daytime robberies increased once people realized that they could get a hefty payday without dealing with windows and safecracking. Bank robberies used to dominate the national news but became so common that it was another local story in the paper. Banks viewed the robberies philosophically, as long as no one was killed. The insurance companies were required to cover the losses, but then they started to raise insurance rates on the banks. The two deaths in Indiana and rising insurance rates forced the banking industry to take action. They would no longer continue to enable this "parasitic class of bank bandits."[225]

After the second murder, the Indiana Bankers Association again pleaded with the legislature to create a state police force. This would be the fifth time. The association put together a bill to be presented to the legislature that sought to address some of the issues that caused previous bills to die. Senator Frank Wright introduced the bill to the 1925 session of the Indiana legislature.

The new state police bill called for the department to be run by three commissioners, serving staggered terms, to be appointed by the governor. In subsequent years, senators were weary of a single superintendent having too much power. Senators were always concerned about the prohibitive cost of having such a large police force. The bill was designed to ensure that no tax increases were needed to fund it. Funding for the new department would come from the $427,500 in the auto theft fund.[226]

The motor vehicle police force, which now consisted of thirty-five officers in 1924, was powerless. Their only concern was enforcing the certificate of title law and auto thefts, but they turned a blind eye to the bank robberies, highwaymen, bootleggers and other criminals terrorizing the state. They didn't even have the power to arrest someone for speeding. Bandits were coming to Indiana because it was ripe for the picking. Indiana had more bank robberies in three years than seven other states that had already implemented a state police force.[227]

The bill called for a department of ninety-seven officers with a defined rank structure. The motor vehicle police would be absorbed into the new state police force. The bill would give the officers full police powers and could make arrests, serve warrants, patrol rural districts and recover stolen automobiles. They were expected to work with county and municipal officers to apprehend criminals.

Like every bill before it, it died in the Senate. Opposition to the bill chiefly came from labor unions. T.N. Taylor, president of the Indiana Federation of Labor, spoke against the bill due to its cost and the possibility that it might be used against organized labor.[228] He was referring to the Great Anthracite Strike in Pennsylvania that led to a nationwide coal shortage and violent unrest that had to be settled by President Theodore Roosevelt.

The strike was the catalyst for the formation of the Pennsylvania State Police, and organized labor viewed it as a private army to be used against them.[229] Instead of passing meaningful legislation that would protect the state's rural citizens, the Senate opted to pass a bill allowing the governor to replace members of the highway commission aligned with his political affiliation. The commission was responsible for the oversight of the motor vehicle police.[230]

Another senator, Charles Batt, proposed that bank robbery should be punishable by death to break up the crime wave.[231] This was criticized, as long prison terms are more of a deterrent than death. It was believed that most juries would not recommend the death penalty.[232] The legislature decided to make bank robbery a thirty-year prison sentence.[233] The Indiana Banking Association realized that it would have to think outside the box since the legislature refused to help.

NATIONAL GUARD

In just two months in 1925, there were thirteen bank robberies with a total loss of $41,230.[234] The crime wave was worsening, and the legislature showed that it would rather appease the labor unions than protect the citizens. Criminals were getting bolder and began to go after banks in the heavily populated cities. Bank robberies in Indianapolis happened so frequently that Mayor Lew Shank ordered an officer be placed in every bank with a sawed-off shotgun. They were instructed with orders to "shoot to kill." Placing an officer in every bank meant pulling officers from their beats when it was hard to fill open positions within the police department. It showed just how serious the crime epidemic had become. Mayor Shank also dissolved the booze squad and reassigned the traffic officers, stressing that capturing bank robbers was more important than arresting bootleggers and speeders.[235]

Recently elected governor Edward Jackson was very concerned about the increasing crime rate and was prepared to take drastic measures to curb the lawlessness throughout the state. He met with representatives of the Indiana Banking Association to formulate a plan. That plan included deploying the Indiana National Guard.[236]

The Indiana National Guard consisted of two infantry and two artillery regiments. Each unit was requested to send twelve volunteers, which would provide an armed force of nearly six hundred men. This would help in guarding the 750 banks throughout the state. Adjutant General William Kershner sent a telegram to the War Department in Washington, D.C., asking for powerful weapons with the "capability of killing a man a mile and a half away."[237]

The idea to use the National Guard was based on the fact that Indiana lacked a state police force, and no organization was large enough to deal with the bank robberies. There were jurisdictional issues, as law enforcement officers would normally turn back at the city or county line to avoid invading another agency's jurisdiction. The soldiers would be able to pursue the suspects as far as they wanted.[238]

The Indiana Bankers Association ultimately rejected the National Guard plan due to cost. Although the state would pay part of the cost, the banks and the banking association would bear most of it. Having the soldiers in the banks for sixty days would cost nearly $100,000, and it was just not practical.[239] So, the banking association decided to pursue the Iowa Plan, which had proven so successful that other states had already adopted it.

IOWA PLAN

Iowa was no different than most other midwestern states. It was experiencing high crime rates, especially bank robberies. The Iowa Banking Association struggled to find a solution. It hired Roscoe Saunders, former chief of police of Des Moines, to address the rising number of bank robberies. Coming from a law enforcement background, he understood that the police were limited in dealing with the problem. He also realized the benefits of using private citizens to combat crime. Reminiscent of the vigilante committees of the mid-1800s, Saunders helped form the Iowa Bankers Protective Association.

Each county would form a vigilante organization that would be made up of volunteer citizens and work in cooperation with law enforcement. The vigilante organizations had legal authority, as they derived their power from the sheriff. Each was deputized, but their authority was limited to bank robberies. A list of the people who were members of the vigilante group was kept on file with the operator. Whenever a bank robbery occurred, an alarm was sounded by the bank. The operator notified the sheriff as well as the members of the vigilante group. They immediately responded, and in most instances, the robber was captured.[240]

The bank vigilantes proved to be a very successful endeavor. In its first year, there were more than 3,800 special deputies equipped with more than 2,000 rifles, 200 sawed-off shotguns and 700,000 rounds of ammunition.[241] The number of bank robberies was reduced from thirty-eight the previous year to two, with a loss of only $2,000. The vigilantes captured seventy-nine bank robbers within the first three years, while four escaped. Of those captured, sixty-four were sentenced to long prison terms, three were acquitted, three had their cases dismissed and six were killed during apprehension.[242] Banks began to see lower insurance rates. Iowa was paying $1 per $1,000 on hand, while Illinois was paying $4.[243]

As the Iowa Plan proved to be successful, other states took notice. The Illinois Banking Association hired Saunders to implement the program there. They experienced a 60 percent decrease within the first six months.[244] Missouri also experimented with the vigilante system, but not on a large scale.[245] California, North Dakota, Oklahoma, Minnesota and Kansas also implemented the plan.[246]

Saunders was invited to address the Indiana Banking Association, which was sold on the idea. The Town of Hope in Bartholomew County had already tried to implement this system about the same time that Iowa was proposing it, but it didn't work out because it lacked the legal authority to act.[247] Under the Iowa plan, the vigilantes would have legal authority under the sheriff.

One of the most important features of the vigilante system was the silent alarm. A burglar alarm manufacturing company designed a system with buttons placed strategically throughout the bank. At the press of a button, alarms would sound at the vigilante posts and police stations without being heard in the bank. This would give the bandits time to complete the robbery while allowing the vigilantes time to assemble. The wires connecting the alarm would be encased in a protective sheath to prevent the robbers from slicing and disarming the alarm.[248]

The banking association created a statewide fund of $100,000 to administer standing rewards of $1,000 for the capture, *dead or alive*, of bank robbers. The vigilantes were given orders to "shoot to kill." Indianapolis police chief Herman Rikhoff told his officers, "Keep your gun handy, and if it comes to a question of shooting, pepper away. And see that you do a good job of it."[249]

Those who opposed the vigilante program mostly came from law enforcement departments. The bank vigilantes were viewed as untrained citizens who were encroaching on their jobs. However, they were also seen as a valuable asset to the state's safety over time. Those who favored the National Guard plan did so because the soldiers were trained marksmen, and there would be less chance of injuring an innocent bystander. Therefore, every vigilante member had to join the National Rifle Association and become a trained marksman.

Indiana held annual shooting contests at Fort Benjamin Harrison in Indianapolis to encourage marksmanship training. Vigilantes around the state would show off their skills using pistols, rifles and shotguns under the supervision of U.S. Army officers. Their performance rivaled that of professional law enforcement agencies and was routinely complimented by the military.[250]

Women were also seen as a vital part of the success of the vigilante system, as it began with them. When a bank robbery occurred, telephone operators notified the vigilante members, who turned the telephone exchange into a "center of operations." The women were compared to Paul Revere as he rode on horseback, warning that the British were coming. Instead of riding on horseback, the women would be using faster communication methods.[251]

Within the first year, the vigilante system was hugely successful. More than seventy counties created a vigilante organization, numbering over two thousand men across the state. Bank robberies had been reduced by 79 percent, and monetary losses had been reduced by 84 percent. There were only seven bank robberies, with a total loss of $14,000. Only one area, Elkhart and Rochester, saw an increase in the amount of money stolen but had reduced the number of bank robberies from two to one.[252]

The vigilante system continued to be improved with new technologies and techniques. Robbers would routinely lock the cashiers in the vault. An alarm system in the vault would sound an audible alarm throughout the town. Vents were installed to prevent suffocation, and a telephone was installed in a hidden location to allow the occupants to communicate. Fire whistles blown at different intervals would signal to outposts that a robbery had occurred. A road blockade system that had been developed by Frank Dunn of Zionsville was implemented. The first vehicle seen traveling down the road would be stopped and used as a blockade while vigilantes took cover with rifles. The bank robbers would either be captured or give chase. Banks had automobiles parked nearby for the use of vigilantes, so they could easily give chase. A signal system was even set up to communicate with neighboring counties to allow for better apprehension.[253]

While attempts to create a state police force had previously gone unanswered in the legislature, they seemed to be coming to a compromise.

The National Crime Commission, created in 1925, was formed to address the rising crime problems nationwide. The commission believed that crime was the responsibility of the states. It urged states to create a commission intent on improving the administration of justice.[254]

In 1927, Indiana became the nineteenth state to implement a statewide crime commission that was as close to a state police force as the banks hoped. The Bureau of Criminal Identification and Investigation, under the secretary of state's office, was created to aid the small towns of Indiana. Through the use of license plates, photographs, fingerprints and body measurements, it would house a database for the identification of criminals. Police departments and banking vigilantes would be given the tools and training to lift fingerprints. This was the beginning of a statewide criminal database in the identification of criminals, and the banking association was credited for getting the legislation passed.[255]

1930 Citizens State Bank Robbery

The life of a bank vigilante was not without its dangers. With the onset of the Great Depression, bank robberies began to increase even in states with vigilante organizations. The benefits outweighed the costs. Indiana experienced another crime wave in December 1930. There were eight bank robberies in nine days. Law enforcement and the vigilantes did their part, killing four of the bandits and capturing another four.[256] But the vigilantes would be forced to experience the death of one of their own.

On Tuesday, December 16, 1930, a gang of bank robbers stormed into the Citizens State Bank in Clinton, the largest city in Vermillion County. The gang was previously responsible for robbing the Tippecanoe Loan & Trust Company on November 1, 1927, in which Lafayette police captain Charles Arman was killed in the line of duty. They were also suspected of robbing the Farmers State Bank in Frankfort on December 3, 1930, for $140,000. The gang was wanted for kidnapping in Des Moines, Iowa, the previous year, and two of the members were wanted as accomplices in the killing of a sheriff and a town marshal in Washington, Iowa, in June 1930 by the Barker-Karpis Gang.[257]

The gang was led by seventy-one-year-old G.W. Landy. Commonly referred to as "Dad," he started his life of crime during the Butch Cassidy and the Sundance Kid era. Landy had been acquitted for a bank robbery in

Vermillion County six years before and had escaped punishment for a gas station robbery in Frankfort.[258] The mastermind of the group was Herman "Baron" Lamm. A German immigrant who had been kicked out of the Prussian army, he viewed bank robbery like a military operation. Known as the father of modern bank robbery, he perfected the "Lamm Technique." It consisted of casing the bank, drawing out floor plans, establishing escape routes and taking meticulous notes. Each member would have a specific job and a strict timetable for the robbery. The technique also included rehearsals with a scaled mock-up of the bank. He was strict on time, and they were only allowed inside the bank for a specific period, regardless of how much money they could get.

Lamm was very successful; his gang raked in more than $1 million during their heists. He was arrested many times and almost always used an alias. He was wanted for the robbery of the Northwestern National Bank in Milwaukee in 1924 for $295,000 and a bank robbery in Superior, Wisconsin, in 1918 and San Francisco in 1917.[259]

The other gang members were twenty-six-year-old Walter Dietrich from Chicago; forty-year-old E.H. Hunter from Terre Haute, considered a daredevil driver; and thirty-eight-year-old James "Oklahoma Jack" Clark of Moberly, Missouri. Clark was the leader of a gang that robbed the National Bank and Trust in Lincoln, Nebraska, on September 17, 1930, of $2,525,000 ($45,636,000 in 2023). At the time, it was the largest bank robbery in U.S. history.[260]

All gang members entered the Citizens State Bank in Clinton except for Hunter, who stayed in the car. They forced the cashier, Lawrence Jackson, to open up the vault. It was time-locked, and they struck Jackson over the head with a revolver out of frustration. They ordered the employees and customers into a prone position on the floor in a back room. Jackson was forced to open a smaller safe, and the robbers escaped with $15,567.

A barber, C.E. Van Sickle, believed that a bank robbery was underway, and he grabbed a shotgun to investigate. As the robbers escaped in their Buick sedan, Hunter, noticing Van Sickle approaching and thinking that he was a vigilante, made a quick U-turn. The vehicle struck the curb, which flattened the tire. They were forced to stop and change the tire a few miles outside of town while being pursued by Clinton police chief Everett Helms, Clinton patrolman Walter Burnsides and a banking vigilante, Ernest Boetto. They engaged in a gun battle while the robbers changed the tire. The police vehicle was hit by more than a dozen bullets, and Burnsides was wounded but stayed in the battle.[261]

Burnsides successfully shot one of their tires, so they abandoned that car for another. That vehicle was equipped with a speed governor, which wouldn't let it go over thirty-five miles per hour, so they had to abandon it again. The robbers stole a cattle truck belonging to Wells Gilbert with him in it. As they approached the small town of Dana, Joseph Walker, who owned a garage and was a Vermillion County banking vigilante, joined in the pursuit. While Herman Lamm drove, Walker took up position in the open-air section of the vehicle. As they began to close the distance, the robbers set up submachine guns in the truck bed. They unleashed a hail of bullets, striking Walker in the abdomen, who was standing up in the vehicle. Lamm immediately turned back around, and Walker was taken to St. Anthony Hospital in Terre Haute, where he was pronounced dead soon after arriving.[262] Joseph Walker became the first known and only banking vigilante to die while carrying out his duties.

The chase crossed into Illinois, and the robbers had to abandon the truck near Scottland when it overheated. They released Gilbert unharmed. They stole a fourth vehicle that had only a gallon of gas. The vehicle gave out near a farm near Sidell, Illinois. The farmer, Leo Moody, opened fire on the vehicle, and the robbers fled into a field while being pursued by a posse and aircraft flying above. After a forty-mile chase across two states, James "Oklahoma Jack" Clark and Walter Dietrich were captured. E.H. Hunter was severely wounded and transported to a hospital in Danville, Illinois, where he died from his injuries two days later.[263] G.W. Landy and Herman Lamm committed suicide.[264] The money was recovered and returned back to the bank.

Dietrich and Clark were charged with first-degree murder. Facing the possibility of death, they were instead sentenced to life imprisonment at the Indiana State Prison.[265] Clinton police chief Everett Helms referred to "Oklahoma Jack" Clark as "America's most dangerous living outlaw."[266] Upon his capture, he was identified by the U.S. Secret Service as having robbed a mint truck of $200,000 in Denver, Colorado, on December 18, 1922.[267] That wasn't the end of the story though.

While in prison, Dietrich and Clark met Harry Pierpont and John Dillinger, two of Indiana's most notorious gangsters. Pierpont and Dillinger had served time together, and Pierpont, whose criminal record dated back to 1921, became a mentor to Dillinger. Pierpont realized that Dietrich and Clark knew Hamm's methods and could be valuable assets to his team. Pierpont set in motion the greatest prison break in Indiana history. Dillinger, who was about to be released, would be allowed to join their gang if he helped them escape. On September 26, 1933, ten inmates escaped the Indiana State Prison.

THE DEMISE OF THE BANKING VIGILANTES

By 1932, bank robbery had become almost unprofitable. Thirty-seven bank robbers were sentenced to prison in one year, and three were killed. There was only one month out of an entire year that the vigilantes failed to capture or convict a bank robber.[268] The vigilantes proved to be very successful in the war against bank robbery.

A number of other factors helped curb bank robbery not only in Indiana but also throughout the country. As a result of the Great Depression, President Franklin Roosevelt passed the Banking Act of 1933, which created the Federal Deposit Insurance Corporation (FDIC). Previously, banks depended on private insurance companies to insure depositors' money, but the money was not always guaranteed. A bank robbery in Fishers in 1930 led to an Indiana Supreme Court case that ruled that the cashier, A.P. Butz, was liable for stolen securities taken during a bank robbery.[269]

The FDIC was meant to restore confidence in the American banking system. Since banks were federally insured, bank robbery was no longer a state crime. It was now a federal crime, under the jurisdiction of the reformed Bureau of Investigation (it became the Federal Bureau of Investigation in 1936), instituted under the leadership of J. Edgar Hoover.[270] In 1933, Indiana governor Paul McNutt issued the Executive Reorganization Act, which combined the motor vehicle bureau, the Bureau of Identification and the Bureau of Investigation into one department, creating the Indiana State Police.[271]

With the FBI chasing the likes of John Dillinger and "Machine Gun" Kelly and Indiana having a statewide police force, the vigilantes slowly faded away. There were still incidents of them engaging in capturing bank robbery suspects, but nothing like it was during the beginning. The shootouts at Fort Benjamin Harrison continued to take place until 1941. After the bombing of Pearl Harbor, the bank vigilante groups began reorganizing to protect banks against saboteurs. Kosciusko County was the first to form, the day after Pearl Harbor, and within a week, forty-one counties had formed vigilante groups.[272] The banking vigilantes exemplify how citizens came together for a common cause to solve a problem in their communities and were highly successful in their endeavors.

CHAPTER 8

HISTORY OF EARLY LAW ENFORCEMENT

Vigilantism grew out of a response to a lack of law enforcement. In the early days, law enforcement was very primitive. The history of law enforcement began with constables, marshals and sheriffs patrolling their communities. As cities grew, the lone constable or marshal wasn't sufficient to provide protection. With the establishment of police departments, it gave birth to the American police officer.

CONSTABLES

Before the automobile, transportation was limited by the speed of the horse. Depending on the size of the county, it could take a whole day to travel to the county seat. The 1851 Indiana Constitution established a more practical form of government through the establishment of townships. Townships provided basic services such as tax collection, property assessments and the operation of schools. Court and marriage ceremonies were performed by the justice of the peace, and law enforcement was the responsibility of constables.[273]

Voters elected constables equal to the number of justices of the peace within their township, serving four-year terms. Sheriffs patrolled the county but rarely employed deputies, as their salaries came from the sheriff's pay.

Sheriffs would usually form posses during times of emergency or when more assistance was required. Larger towns would normally have a marshal to keep law and order. Therefore, the rural areas outside of cities and towns depended on constables for protection.[274]

Constables' income derived from fees for various services: serving warrants and subpoenas, attending jury trials, summoning juries, posting advertisements and selling property. Constables also earned money for mileage. In 1897, the Indiana legislature identified twenty-eight ways that constables could earn money, none over one dollar. They could make more money from mileage alone than from their services. Constables began exchanging business with one another so they could make more money.[275]

Constables sometimes found illegal ways to make money at the expense of the public. In 1907, four constables from Haughville, a city annexed by Indianapolis in 1897, were arrested for extortion, blackmail, embezzlement and larceny. Judge Grant Hollingsworth was forced to close up his court amid the revelations that his constables were shaking down the public and overcharging court fees.[276] In 1931, constables in Warren Township in Indianapolis held "kangaroo courts," and citizens paid fines for crimes that they didn't commit.[277]

Amid complaints that constables were abusing their authority, the Indiana legislature in 1939 began to limit their powers. They were prohibited from arresting motorists without a warrant. Township officials argued that the law was unconstitutional and that it stripped them of powers granted by the state constitution. However, the law was upheld by the Indiana Supreme Court.[278] The number of constables today has mostly dwindled. Constables can be found in townships that operate small claims courts. They have law enforcement powers to carry out the court's orders.

The first known law enforcement officer killed in Indiana was Constable Robert Murphy. Murphy was serving a warrant on a seventy-five-year-old man for assaulting his female neighbor in Bath Township in Franklin County. The suspect met him at the door, carrying a knife and thrusting it into his left side. Murphy succumbed to his wounds eight days later, on November 11, 1824. The suspect was convicted of first-degree murder and sentenced to death. He was pardoned six months later by Governor James B. Ray as he stood on the gallows awaiting his death.[279]

MARSHALS

While constables were responsible for the unincorporated areas of the townships, marshals were responsible for the cities and towns. Marshals were either elected or appointed. In the early days, elections were held only if a candidate had a challenger. If the candidates were unopposed, no election was held, mainly due to the high cost of holding elections. Marshals received compensation for the fees that they collected. In some localities like Fishers, in 1891, the council opted to give the marshal a yearly salary of twenty-five dollars. A marshal was mostly a part-time position, as many were farmers or businesspeople. The position was plagued by high turnover. In 1907, marshals were allowed to appoint deputies.[280]

The first known marshal killed in Indiana was Bedford marshal George Carney on January 20, 1875. He was shot and killed when he interrupted a burglary at a local drugstore. After a shootout with the town marshal, both men escaped but were captured in Olney, Illinois. They were both sentenced to life in prison.[281]

SHERIFF

Sheriff is the oldest law enforcement position, dating back to England in 871. The word is derived from the Anglo-Saxon term *shire-reeve*. A shire was the forerunner of the modern county, and *reeve* referred to chief. In 871, King Alfred the Great entrusted the sheriff to maintain law and order within their county. Citizens were legally obligated to assist the sheriff in keeping the peace. That principle of direct citizen participation survives today as *posse comitatus*.[282]

When the colonists came to America, the role of sheriff came with them. The first sheriff in the United States was Captain William Stone, appointed in 1634 for the shire of Northhampton in the Virginia Colony. William Waters became the first elected sheriff in the United States from the same shire in 1652.[283] In 1790, Colonel John Small was appointed as the first sheriff in the newly formed Knox County, Indiana. Having fought in the Revolutionary War, he moved to Vincennes shortly after the war from Pennsylvania. He operated a local tavern that would serve as the first county courthouse. Today, Knox County deputies honor Colonel John Small with a patch on its uniform reading, "First in Indiana—1790."[284]

The sheriff's responsibilities are largely unchanged from its roots in England. The sheriff is expected to keep the peace, maintain the jails, serve civil papers and arrest fugitives. When Indiana became a state in 1816, every county had an elected sheriff. The direct election of the sheriff is what separates it from other law enforcement positions. In most states, electing a sheriff is a constitutional requirement. Of the 3,083 sheriffs in the United States, 98 percent are elected.[285]

The sheriff has been referred to as the county's most powerful law enforcement officer. In most jurisdictions, the sheriff can be arrested only by the county coroner, another tradition brought over from England. During frontier times, the sheriff was not that effective. It would take a long time to cover the county on horseback. The sheriff couldn't cross county lines to pursue suspects. For decades, sheriff's deputies were paid from the sheriff's salary instead of the county treasury. For this reason, the sheriff very rarely employed deputies.

The first sheriff to be killed in the line of duty in Indiana was William Gresham on January 23, 1834, in Harrison County. He was shot and killed while attempting to serve an arrest warrant. The local constable could not serve it, so it fell on Gresham. The suspect was arrested and convicted of manslaughter. He was sentenced to twenty-one years in prison and fined $1,000. The suspect was pardoned by the governor in 1840 and had the fine remitted. Gresham was killed in his first year of being sheriff.[286]

BIRTH OF THE POLICE OFFICER

As the state's population grew, a city marshal became insufficient to protect some cities and towns. More officers were needed, which led to the creation of police departments. In 1857, Indianapolis was the first city in the state to have a police department after two previous attempts failed.[287] By 1875, Indianapolis had sixty-two patrolmen, along with a sheriff and five deputies, covering a city of eighty thousand people.[288]

Police departments were a tool of political patronage and control, and that was evident in 1883 with the passage of the metropolitan police law. Democrats had taken control of the General Assembly and most state offices. The governor, Albert G. Porter, was a Republican elected in 1880. Democrats wanted to take the Indianapolis Police Department out of Republican control. The law created a board consisting of the governor, secretary of state, state auditor and state treasurer, the latter three being Democrats. The board had the power to select the superintendent and oversaw the hiring and firing of officers. The law also provided for one officer per one thousand people, and the force had to have an equal number of Republicans and Democrats.[289]

In 1889, Republicans had taken over the top state offices, and the board had a Republican majority. The Democratic-controlled legislature tried to dissolve the board and give the appointing power to the General Assembly. However, the Indiana Supreme Court struck that down as unconstitutional. At the time, the law applied only to two cities, Indianapolis and Evansville. That's because, in 1891, the legislature amended the law to apply to cities with more than fourteen thousand schoolchildren. This was done specifically to exclude Fort Wayne, which was a Democratic city, and it was allowed to govern itself. Terre Haute, a Republican city, had a smaller population than Fort Wayne, but it had more schoolchildren. The legislature seized on this to be able to control Republican cities.[290] That same year, Indianapolis was granted a special charter that replaced the metropolitan police board with a Board of Public Safety. Appointees to the board were no longer the responsibility of the governor but rather the mayor.[291]

In 1893, the law was amended again to include cities of not more than 35,000 nor less than 10,000 population. During the 1890 census, Fort Wayne exceeded 35,000 people by 393 and was not subject to the law. In 1897, Republicans took back control of the legislature. The power to appoint police boards was back in the hands of the governor. Two members would be of one party and one member of the other. Therefore, the board would be whatever political party the governor was. By 1904, the metropolitan police law was being applied to Anderson, Elkhart, Elwood, Hammond, Jeffersonville, Kokomo, Lafayette, Logansport, Michigan City, Muncie, Marion, New Albany, Richmond and Vincennes.[292]

Politics continued to plague police departments. In 1935, the legislature passed the police merit law to remove politics from the police and increase its effectiveness. It wasn't uncommon for half the department to be out of a job when different political parties took over. Officers found themselves unemployed for no better reason than their political affiliation. Milwaukee's police force was considered a model of efficiency because it kept politics out of the department by giving the chief of police absolute power. A board chose the chief upon approval by the mayor and city council. Milwaukee had only two police chiefs over a forty-six-year period. Those things that worked so well for Milwaukee were applied in Indiana. The only problem with the new law was that it applied only to Indianapolis.[293]

In 1957, the legislature passed a police merit law that would only apply to Evansville. It came with some controversy, as the legislation set a mandatory retirement age of sixty-five. Evansville's oldest officer, Joe Currigan, seventy-one, was forced out after being an officer for forty-two years.[294] It also required that all officers with rank be re-tested to see if they would retain their rank. Promotions were a source of political patronage for a long time, and the new merit law would provide a more equitable system. Lawsuits were filed against the merit law, but it was held to be constitutional.

By 1967, it was estimated that nearly 30 percent of the 7,200 law enforcement officers in the state had no formal police training.[295] Only five major cities provided training to their officers: Indianapolis, Gary, Fort Wayne, South Bend and Evansville. The legislature passed a bill creating the Indiana Law Enforcement Academy. Robert O'Neal, Indiana State Police superintendent, called it "the greatest thing that ever happened to Indiana law enforcement."[296] In 1969, 99 officers graduated from the first academy class held at the Indiana Central College (now the University of Indianapolis).[297] The academy moved to Indiana University in Bloomington from 1969 to 1975 until its permanent facility in Plainfield was completed.[298]

MERCHANT POLICE

In larger cities like Indianapolis, the business districts lacked adequate protection from the city police force. In 1881, fifty-one officers patrolled a city that was seventeen square miles. Business merchants created a separate police force that would be dedicated to protecting businesses. The Merchant Police Force was first established in Indianapolis in 1865 by Daniel Coquillard. It began with nine officers; by 1900, it had grown to fifty-seven. The merchant and city police had the same arrest powers but differed in many ways.

The city police force was paid out of the city treasury, while merchant police derived their salary from the merchants whose businesses they patrolled. The officer and the merchant agreed on a fixed amount, ranging from $0.25 to $5.00 per week, based on the level of protection. The average salary of a merchant officer in 1886 was $1,000 ($32,000 in 2023). Some city officers would join the merchant police because it could be more lucrative than a flat salary paid by the city. The officers paid dues, the funds of which were used to help officers when they were sick.[299] The city police force was governed by three commissioners who appointed a superintendent to oversee the department. The merchant police have no such hierarchy, and its highest rank was a captain and a lieutenant.[300]

Indianapolis was broken down into seventeen districts, with one officer in each district by day and two officers at night. An advantage of the merchant police was that they were on patrol all night from 7:00 p.m. until daylight. If a city officer arrested an individual, they would be off their beat for a considerable time. When merchant officers make an arrest, they can hand the person off to the city police force, allowing them to stay on their beat. They were highly successful, arresting hundreds of people yearly, putting out fires and saving business owners money.

The Board of Public Safety governed the city and the merchant police forces. The board attempted numerous times to reorganize the merchant police on a partisan basis. In 1900, twenty-three of the fifty-seven members of the merchant police resigned after the board forced them to wear uniforms. Merchant police patrolled in civilian clothes as the best way to surprise criminals. When the board threatened to revoke their police powers, they resigned and formed a new organization, the Indianapolis Merchant Detectives Association. The members received their police powers from the Marion County commissioners, as provided for by state law.[301]

Business districts in other major cities—like Evansville, Seymour and South Bend—began to implement merchant police. Merchant police have all but disappeared and today resemble private security companies like Trident and Securitas.

Three merchant police officers were killed in Indiana: John L. Watterson, Indianapolis (1893); George W. Lee, Alexandria (1899); and Edward Keasey, Ligonier (1934). Watterson was stabbed and beaten to death by three suspects after he interrupted a burglary at a meat market in downtown Indianapolis. He was able to injure one of the suspects with his revolver. He chased the men one block before collapsing. Two suspects were arrested but later released for lack of evidence. No one was ever charged with his murder. Watterson was the first African American officer killed in Indiana.

CHAPTER 9

FEDERAL GOVERNMENT

Law and order was almost exclusively the jurisdiction of the state and local governments. The federal government was limited in its ability to enforce laws. The U.S. Constitution technically prohibits a federal police force. The framers of the Constitution intended to leave law enforcement decentralized and in the hands of the states, as it was considered the best way to maintain a democratic government.[302] However, the framers did not envision how technological innovations would transform daily life. The mobility of Americans to travel greater distances than ever before was made possible by the automobile. But it also hampered the ability of state and local governments to enforce laws. The federal government realized that there was a need for federal agencies to have law enforcement responsibilities. Currently, there are more than sixty-five different federal law enforcement agencies; however, they are limited in what they investigate.

U.S. MARSHAL SERVICE

The U.S. Marshal Service is the country's oldest federal law enforcement agency. The service was created by the Judiciary Act of 1789, which also created the U.S. Supreme Court. It was given extensive authority to support the federal courts in its districts. It did this by serving subpoenas, writs, warrants and the arrests of prisoners. To counter the marshals' extensive authority, Congress imposed four-year renewable terms, serving at the pleasure of the president. The U.S. marshals helped to bring order to areas of the United States that had little to no government. They were also the only point of contact between the federal government and local communities.[303]

Indiana had a federal presence before it became a state on December 11, 1816. President James Madison appointed John Vawter the first U.S. marshal for Indiana on July 27, 1813, when it was the Territory of Indiana. Upon it being admitted as a state, Vawter was appointed by President James Monroe as the first marshal for the District of Indiana. (Indiana would be divided into a northern and southern district in 1928.) Vawter was reappointed a fourth time by President John Quincy Adams.[304] Vawter settled in Madison, Indiana, in 1807 from Virginia. He became the first justice of the peace and sheriff of Jefferson County. He left Madison in 1815 and, while a U.S. marshal, founded the town of Vernon in Jennings County. Today, it is the smallest county seat in Indiana.[305]

U.S. Secret Service

The country was flooded with counterfeit currency at the close of the Civil War. The counterfeiters were usually well known, but it was difficult to get the necessary evidence against them for a conviction. The government created the U.S. Secret Service on July 5, 1865, under its first chief, William P. Wood. A division of the Treasury Department, its main purpose was investigating counterfeit currency. While there was some animosity between the federal government and the local communities, one of the earliest policies of the Secret Service was the cooperation with the local police forces.[306]

The Secret Service divided the country into districts. Indiana, Ohio and Kentucky made up one district, with its headquarters in Cincinnati. In 1875, Estes G. Rathbone, a native of Wellsville, New York, was appointed the district chief. In 1874, the mayor asked Rathbone to investigate the passing of counterfeit currency in the city, although he had no law enforcement experience. He proved successful, and after relaying his findings to Washington, the Secret Service arrested eight individuals. The Secret Service was impressed with his work, and he was offered a position in the service. After a brief stint in Philadelphia, he was transferred to Cincinnati.[307]

Rathbone became legendary for capturing two of the country's most notorious counterfeiters. Pete McCartney was regarded as the best counterfeiter in the United States. He earned the nickname "King of the Coniakers" (a term used to describe someone who makes counterfeit currency). Growing up on a farm, he had a keen sense for mechanical engineering, but farm life was too dull. He began his life of crime as a burglar but wasn't very good at it. After being sent to prison at a young age, he learned the art of counterfeiting. He studied every science discipline and became a skilled chemist and toolmaker. He made his own engraving plates and tools. He began to counterfeit money and bonds during and after the Civil War. His counterfeits were so perfect that it was almost impossible to identify them.[308] His most successful work was a counterfeit $1,000 bond that even fooled the U.S. Treasury Department. The holder of the genuine bond was arrested and charged with counterfeiting.[309]

In December 1875, McCartney was captured in St. Louis after being shot by a Secret Service agent. Before he could be tried, he escaped from jail.[310] After learning how to engrave, he also became skilled at making skeleton keys, which made him highly sought after by criminals. His ability to escape added to his reputation.[311] Realizing how close he came to being killed, he fled Missouri for Richmond, Indiana.

During the summer of 1876, the Richmond city marshal arrested McCartney for passing a $20 counterfeit bill. McCartney tried to bribe the marshal to let him go with $2,800 of genuine currency, but the marshal refused. It was soon discovered that counterfeit bills had been passed all over town. Rathbone arrived in Richmond from Cincinnati and immediately recognized him. Given his penchant for escaping, McCartney was guarded until his trial. He pleaded guilty to one count of possession of counterfeit treasury notes with the intent to defraud. The other charges against him were dismissed in exchange for surrendering the plates used to make the bills. He received a fifteen-year sentence in the Indiana State Prison.[312]

Indiana passed a state law in 1883 allowing credit for good behavior. McCartney was released in 1887 after serving eleven years.[313] As soon as he was released, he was re-arrested on a twenty-year-old counterfeit charge and transported to Springfield, Illinois. He was soon released, as the statute of limitations had expired.[314] In 1888, he moved to New Orleans with his younger daughter, but it didn't take long for him to fall back into his old ways. He was arrested for passing counterfeit bills and sentenced to ten years. He was imprisoned at the Federal Penitentiary in Columbus, Ohio, but he died after only serving two years.[315] The king of counterfeiters was dead, but his protégé would carry on his legacy.

Miles Ogle, also a New York native, grew up in a life of crime. His father was a career criminal. In 1862, his father purchased a flatboat near Cincinnati. His wife and two sons, Miles and John, set out on the Ohio River to rob residents along the river. On April 13, 1862, Evansville constable John Welch attempted to arrest Miles Ogle. Knowing that he was on the boat, he sent for another officer but approached the boat without waiting. As he approached, a dog began barking, attracting Ogle's mother's attention. Welch drew his revolver, and Ogle told his mother, "Let him in; I'll kill him if he comes." As the door opened and Welch entered, Ogle fired two shots from a double-barrel shotgun. Welch was shot in the right arm and the chest. Ogle's mother also struck Welch with a stick. Ogle escaped down the river but was eventually captured.[316] He served five years in the Indiana State Prison in Jeffersonville for manslaughter.[317] Welch was the fourth officer killed in the line of duty in Indiana and Evansville's first fallen officer.

After being released from prison, Ogle joined the Reno Gang from Seymour, Indiana. In 1868, Ogle and three others were arrested in Council Bluffs, Iowa, for robbing the treasurers' offices in six counties. They escaped from jail, but not before scribbling in chalk "April Fool" on the wall. They fled to Seymour, where Ogle participated in a train robbery of the Adams Express, which netted more than $90,000 ($1.9 million in 2023) and made national headlines. Ten members of the gang, including the three Reno brothers, were eventually lynched. Although Ogle was arrested at Seymour, he managed to escape custody and death.[318]

Shortly after the lynchings, Ogle met McCartney, who was hiding out in Indiana. Ogle became a protégé to the master counterfeiter. In 1871, they created an almost identical $5 plate and flooded the country with counterfeits. Ogle was so impressed with the work that he stole $75,000 of the fake currency and sold it to "shovers" (a term for people who pass counterfeit currency) in Cincinnati. He was eventually arrested in Philadelphia and put in jail. He agreed to work with the government in exchange for his freedom. He acted as a spy, turning in other counterfeiters, which helped him eliminate his competition. He didn't like living an honest life or being a spy and went back to his old ways.[319]

He quickly became one of the most well-known and skilled counterfeiters in the United States, if not the world. His counterfeiting was considered superior to McCarthy's. After successfully sending McCarthy to prison in Indiana, Agent Rathbone set his eyes on Ogle. After the Secret Service shut his operation down in Philadelphia, Ogle went back to Cincinnati. He owned a livery stable, which became a front for his counterfeiting business. Rathbone followed him to Pittsburgh, where he was arrested. In his possession, Ogle had $7,000 in counterfeit currency, primarily for Indiana banks. (During this time, state banks issued their own currency.) He had plates for Indiana banks in Richmond, Lafayette and Muncie and the plate to make fifty-cent coins.[320] Ogle was sentenced to eight years in the Western Penitentiary in Pittsburgh.[321]

Ogle was released from prison in July 1883. He was immediately arrested upon his release for a counterfeiting charge in Cincinnati. However, the charge was dismissed at his wife's pleading and the promise to live a reformed life. Within three months, he was back to his old ways. Michael Bauer had taken over the Cincinnati office in 1885 after Rathbone became the chief of the special examination office of the U.S. Pension Office. Bauer received information that Ogle was in Memphis, Tennessee, trying to pass counterfeit currency.[322]

In September 1883, Ogle, with his brother, purchased a flatboat in Parkersburg, West Virginia. Ogle built a printing shop on the boat, while his brother acted as a lookout. By the time the boat arrived in Cairo, Illinois, Ogle had $149,000 in $20 silver certificates to be sold to dealers. Bauer set up an undercover operation that resulted in the arrest of Ogle. He tried to bribe the chief of police with $5,000 in genuine currency to let him go, but the chief refused. The arrest yielded all his tools, and his work was almost superior to what the government could do. Bauer recovered almost $180,000 in counterfeit currency and said that Ogle "showed an almost unexampled skill and astuteness."[323] In exchange for turning over his tools and pleading guilty, he was sentenced to six years in the Southern Penitentiary in Chester, Illinois.[324]

In the same way that McCarthy catapulted Rathbone's career, Ogle did the same for Bauer. Ogle was released from prison in April 1889, and he once again was caught counterfeiting in Memphis. This time, the judge gave him the maximum sentence, fifteen years in the federal penitentiary in Columbus, Ohio. His teacher, McCartney, was in the same prison and died shortly after his arrival.[325] Ogle served ten years before he was released in June 1900 due to being an invalid. He died a few weeks later, and one of the most skillful counterfeiters in U.S. history faded from history.[326]

With the assassination of President William McKinley in 1901, the Secret Service took on the added responsibility of being the president's bodyguard. The Secret Service lived up to its name, as the organization's inner workings were unknown. It was commonly referred to as the "Black Cabinet." Other federal departments had no investigative unit, so agents were loaned out.

The interior department used them to investigate land fraud cases, the agricultural department used them to uncover an insider trading scheme involving cotton and the Justice Department for a variety of investigations.[327] In 1908, Congress passed a bill prohibiting the Secret Service from performing any investigations that did not deal with counterfeiting or presidential protection.[328] Because of this, the Justice Department created the Bureau of Investigation (later renamed the Federal Bureau of Investigation).

FEDERAL BUREAU OF INVESTIGATION

After Congress prohibited the use of Secret Service agents by other federal departments, Attorney General Charles Bonaparte created a small investigative service within the Department of Justice. It consisted of thirty-four agents, nine of whom belonged to the Secret Service, under the leadership of its first chief, Stanley Finch. Bonaparte's successor, George Wickersham, gave the agents their first name, the Bureau of Investigation (BOI).[329]

One of the first major responsibilities of the BOI was investigating the "white slave trade." In January 1910, newly elected New York City district attorney Charles Whitman convened a grand jury to investigate sex trafficking. New York City had become a clearinghouse for trafficking in young women from all around the country. John D. Rockefeller Jr. was appointed as foreman of the grand jury.[330]

The grand jury investigation resulted in numerous indictments and the recovery of girls who had been trafficked from as far as Juneau, Alaska. New York City's Tenderloin District had become a haven for brothels, where dealers purchased underage girls for five dollars.[331] One of the victims was nineteen-year-old Stella Freeland from Brazil, Indiana, who testified against her captors. She explained how she was lured into marriage under false pretenses and then sold into slavery. She was deprived of her clothes and subjected to horrible abuse.[332]

It was estimated that between fifteen thousand and twenty thousand girls were victims of sex trafficking annually. Some states began to pass legislation to curb trafficking. Railroad companies got involved by refusing to sell tickets for potential victims. Traffickers would defray the cost of a ticket as bait as they lured their victims into the slave trade.[333] Congressman James Mann of Illinois proposed a federal solution to the problem. On June 25, 1910, Congress passed the White-Slave Traffic Act, or Mann Act, which made it a felony to engage in the interstate or foreign commerce of any woman or girl for prostitution or immoral purposes.[334]

With its limited number of agents, the BOI was tasked with enforcing the Mann Act. The first prosecution under the new law in Indiana took place in Evansville on October 28, 1910. Parson Wyatt, an oil worker from Omaha, Illinois, lured Nellie Kennedy to Evansville. They stayed in a hotel together for a week before he tried to leave her at a brothel run by two women. U.S. District Attorney Charles W. Miller traveled from Indianapolis to prosecute the case.[335]

The BOI proved to be a success. By 1914, it had convicted nearly 1,000 people involved in the white slave trade. The agency began to take on international issues, enforcing neutrality violations with Mexico with agents on the border and inside the country.[336] With a host of other domestic investigations responsibilities, the agency personnel increased to 360 agents. With the expansion of the bureau, Indiana received its first field office in June 1914, with its headquarters in Indianapolis. Previously, investigations in Indiana were assigned to agents in surrounding states. The first agent assigned to the Indianapolis field office was A.F. Kearney, a native of Maquoketa, Iowa, who was first appointed as a special agent in November 1913.[337]

Kearney's tenure in Indianapolis was brief, and the outbreak of war in Europe dominated it. Almost immediately after the war started, certain manufacturers began to profit off the war by raising prices on goods that included sugar, flour and cotton.[338] For instance, one hundred pounds of sugar increased from $4.30 to $7.52, and brokers refused to sell unless the buyer agreed not to lower the price.[339] A federal investigation was launched under the direction of U.S. District Attorney Milton W. Mangus. Agents with the BOI and the Internal Revenue Service and food inspectors with the U.S. Department of Agriculture cooperated to curb the price hikes. Kearney resigned his post in December 1914 to make an unsuccessful run for mayor in Maquoketa.[340]

Robert Ramsey took over in Indianapolis.[341] He served in the post for two years, and a major election fraud investigation in Terre Haute dominated his tenure. Mayor Donn Roberts masterminded an election fraud scheme that resulted in fraudulent ballots and intimidated citizens not to vote. The investigation led to the arrests of 116 people and sent Roberts to prison for three and a half years.[342]

Ramsey left his position to return to his alma mater, Washington and Lee University.[343] George Murdock took over just as the United States entered

World War I. With the United States severing diplomatic relations with Germany, German residents living in the United States came under intense surveillance. Germans were forbidden to enter restricted zones throughout the country, including armories, military reservations and government buildings. Germans living in Indiana had to go to Indianapolis to get a permit to live or work in certain restricted areas, sometimes including entire cities.[344] Murdock required that German residents had to supply a bond before they were allowed to enter a restricted zone.[345]

In 1917, the federal government passed the Selective Service Act to raise a national army through conscription. There were 120,000 soldiers in the regular army, and Congress, realizing that this was not enough to fight a war, passed a law allowing President Woodrow Wilson to increase the military temporarily. All men between the ages of twenty-one and thirty-one were required to register for the draft.[346] The BOI and the local authorities would seek out those who refused to register. Failing to register would almost certainly ensure that the person would be moved to the top of the list.[347] The BOI was also tasked with going after those who failed to report for duty, as they were classified as deserters.[348] In extreme cases, Oklahoma arrested nearly 300 people engaging in anti-draft rioting and charged them with espionage, an offense punishable by death.[349]

The BOI was inundated with investigating all manners of espionage. When German agents were suspected of stealing the draft list containing 2,691 names for the first selection of the draft from the Marion County conscription office, the BOI took over the investigation.[350] During this time, the U.S. government declared that the book *Finished Mystery* by Charles Taze Russell violated the espionage law. It was written by a minister and founder of the Bible Student Movement (later it split into Jehovah's Witnesses), and the government considered the book to be dangerous and disloyal German propaganda.[351] Throughout Indiana, thousands of copies were either turned in voluntarily or seized by BOI agents.[352]

After the war ended in 1918, the BOI faced new challenges and changes. In 1920, the United States went dry as Prohibition went into effect (Indiana went dry in 1918). In 1921, J. Edgar Hoover was appointed deputy director, and Edward L. Osborne, former police chief of Lafayette, took over the Indianapolis field office.[353] In 1922, Alaska P. Davidson became the first female agent in the United States. That same year, Indiana made history with the appointment of the first African American federal agent in the state, Earl F. Titus. A former Indianapolis police officer, he was dismissed from the department due to political reasons. Senator Harry

New successfully lobbied for his appointment to become the third African American BOI officer in the country.[354]

After the Teapot Dome scandal engulfed the Harding administration, Hoover was appointed director of the bureau in 1924. The agency had nearly 650 employees, including 441 agents. Hoover was determined to reorganize the bureau to make it a professional and effective law enforcement agency. By 1929, the bureau had downsized to 339 agents, and field offices were consolidated.[355] The Indianapolis field office closed, and responsibility for the state was transferred to the Cincinnati field office.[356] With the closure of the field office, Osborne left the federal government to become the first chief of the Indiana Bureau of Criminal Investigation and Identification.[357]

In June 1934, Director Hoover approved the establishment of six new field offices: Indianapolis, Denver, Omaha, Nashville, Buffalo and Little Rock.[358] The reestablishment of the Indianapolis field office coincided with the federal government's active pursuit of John Dillinger. Reed E. Vetterli, former chief of the San Francisco office, was put in charge of the Indiana office. He was credited with the arrest and conviction of George (Machine Gun) Kelly.[359] A few months after Dillinger was killed in Chicago, Vetterli was replaced with H.H. Reinecke, who was part of the Chicago field office that took an active part in the Dillinger campaign.[360] In 1935, the agency was renamed the Federal Bureau of Investigation (FBI).

NELSON KLEIN

On August 16, 1935, an FBI agent, Nelson Klein, became the first FBI agent to be killed in the line of duty in Indiana. Assigned to the Cincinnati field office, he was killed attempting to arrest a Kentucky moonshiner, George Barrett, for auto theft. Since 1931, Barrett had been dealing in stolen automobiles and was under surveillance by the FBI. He operated his illegitimate business from his home in Hamilton, Ohio. He had a brother who lived in College Corner, Ohio, where Barrett also made a lot of transactions. After he was alerted that the FBI was looking for him, he decided to go to Texas. Before leaving, he went to College Corner to retrieve a pistol at his brother's house to take to Texas.

Klein and Agent Donald McGovern attempted to arrest Barrett as he exited the house, and a gun battle ensued. Klein was shot five times but returned fire and struck Barrett in the legs. Klein was pronounced dead at the scene, and Barrett was transported to a hospital in Hamilton, Ohio. Barrett was tried for murder, but the issue was *where* he would be tried. College Corner is a unique city in that it is split between Indiana and Ohio. It was determined that Klein's murder took place a few feet inside Indiana, so Barrett's trial would be held in Indianapolis.[361]

In 1934, after Dillinger's exploits, Congress passed a law allowing for death by hanging for any person accused of murdering a federal agent. John Paul Chase, associate of "Baby Face" Nelson, was the first person to be tried under the new law when he murdered Agent Samuel Cowley and Herman Hollis. The Chicago jury recommended mercy, and he was spared the death penalty and sent to Alcatraz.[362] Barrett would not be shown the same mercy and was sentenced to death.

Barrett was executed by hanging on March 24, 1936, at the gallows erected at the Marion County Jail.[363] It had been nearly forty years since the last hanging in Indiana, when George Williams was executed on February 8, 1907, convicted of killing Indianapolis police officer Edward Pettiford. Indiana had replaced hanging with the electric chair in 1913.[364] Senator Frederick Van Nuys of Indiana amended the law so that in the future, hanging would be replaced with whatever method the state provides, and the execution would be carried out at the state prison.[365]

The address of the FBI field office in Indianapolis was named in Klein's honor. His son, Nelson B. Klein Jr., became an FBI agent and was also killed in the line of duty in 1969 in an on-duty accident.

BUREAU OF PROHIBITION

On April 2, 1918, Indiana became the twenty-fifth state to prohibit alcohol and go dry. Congress had already passed the Eighteenth Amendment prohibiting alcohol on December 18, 1917, but it required three-fourths of the state legislatures to ratify it. Indiana ratified it on January 14, 1919. Two days later, Nebraska ratified it, becoming the thirty-sixth state to ratify the amendment and achieving the necessary three-fourths majority. Prohibition officially began on January 16, 1920, and the Volstead Act provided the means to enforce the amendment.[366]

The Volstead Act created the Bureau of Prohibition, an Internal Revenue Service (IRS) unit within the Department of the Treasury. This new unit would have a force of 1,200 personnel, with each state having a

Prohibition director. The director, along with Prohibition agents, would be responsible for surveillance and enforcement of anyone who manufactured, sold or transported alcohol.[367] Charles J. Orbison was appointed as the first prohibition director in Indiana and would have two headquarters locations, Indianapolis and Hammond.[368]

Orbison's first task was to rectify differences between federal and state Prohibition laws. When Indiana passed its prohibition law in 1918, producing wine or cider for domestic consumption was legal. Under federal law, it prohibited all alcoholic beverages that exceeded 0.5 percent, regardless of the purpose. Orbison ruled that state law conflicted with federal law.[369] However, at the same time, federal law allowed one pint of liquor every ten days for medicinal purposes.[370] That included whiskey for many states, but Indiana law only allowed grain alcohol to be dispensed with a doctor's prescription. The world was still battling the 1918 influenza pandemic that claimed an estimated 50 million deaths, with 675,000 deaths in the United States.[371] Liquor was prescribed as a cure for the flu. Orbison ruled that only grain alcohol could be prescribed, while whiskey and other intoxicating liquors would be prohibited in accordance with state law.[372]

The first major raid occurred in June 1920 in South Bend, which had gained national attention as a major city for trafficking alcohol and narcotics. While the Prohibition unit wanted to cooperate with the local authorities, the reality is that most of them could not be trusted. While prohibition may have been the law of the land, many did not agree with it, including those who were tasked to enforce it. More than forty federal agents, operating in secrecy, took control of the telephone and telegraph company so word of the operation would not leak out. The first that the police or the public was made aware of the operation was in the paper published shortly after the first arrest. It resulted in the arrest of fifteen people.[373]

It wasn't just the local authorities who were corrupt—many within the Prohibition unit were too. In January 1921, Orbison was discovered to have been dispensing seized whiskey held by the Indianapolis police department to family and friends. Letters addressed "Dear Jerry" (referencing Indianapolis police chief Jerry Kinney) and signed "Your Friend" (referencing Orbison) ordered that whiskey be delivered to various people for medicinal purposes. The letters served as a prescription, and Orbison used Dr. Thomas Beasley's name as authorizing it. However, Beasley refuted this and claimed that he had never met Orbison or any people who supposedly had prescriptions.

The whiskey was dispensed for various medicinal reasons, some highly questionable: colds, pneumonia, whooping cough, anemia, childbirth, asthma, tuberculosis, anxiety, exhaustion, cancer and stomach trouble. Even if it was a valid medical reason, state law did not allow the whiskey to be dispensed. Some of the whiskey was dispensed for non-medical reasons such as auto accidents, a dentist who needed it to sterilize his equipment, as a replacement after a neighbor borrowed it and "emergencies."[374] Some of the people who received the whiskey were agents, including Orbison himself, who received three quarts of whiskey for his work as prohibition director.[375] Judge Will Sparks, from Rush County, was appointed a special judge in Marion County to hear a case that upheld the state law prohibiting druggists from selling whiskey on a physician's prescription. Sparks were found to have requested a quart of whiskey for an eighty-five-year-old woman suffering from cancer.[376]

Nearly 150 "Dear Jerry" letters were discovered, prompting a federal investigation and convening a federal grand jury. In total, 127 quarts, 49 pints and 2 half pints were dispensed from the property room of the Indianapolis Police Department. Orbison maintained that he was innocent of any wrongdoing. His actions were for the betterment of humanity and to relieve suffering. While there is no evidence that he profited from the distribution of illegal whiskey, he violated the Volstead Act and Indiana law, the same laws he was sworn to enforce.[377]

After the scandal, Bert Morgan replaced Orbison as state prohibition director. Upon taking office, Indiana was reorganized as a separate enforcement district, having previously been under the supervision of the Chicago field office.[378]

On April 16, 1923, the Prohibition unit in Indiana suffered its first line of duty death. Before Prohibition, the Hammond Distillery was the second-largest distillery in the state. When the distillery closed its doors, there were an estimated nine hundred barrels of whiskey valued at $1.3 million inside, and it was rumored to have some of the oldest whiskey in the country.[379] It was the site of many break-ins, and agents were stationed at the distillery to keep the inventory safe. In the early morning hours, six men took an agent hostage as he arrived to relieve the night shift. They forced the agent to tell Agent Robert Anderson to come to the gate. When Anderson arrived, he pulled his revolver after noticing that the other agent had been taken hostage. The bandits shot and killed Agent Anderson. Anderson's killer, Joe Soltos, was a Chicago gangster nicknamed the "Beer Baron." He was acquitted at trial when the other federal agent taken hostage couldn't clearly identify who killed Anderson. A few months later, he was acquitted of another murder. Al Capone eventually put him out of business.[380]

While Morgan proved to be a far better director than his predecessor, he was replaced in 1924 for political reasons. Morgan was an efficient public servant who believed in Prohibition and believed in the just enforcement of the law.[381] He also had the support of Senator Harry New, but he left that position in 1923 to become postmaster general. New and Senator James Watson, both Republicans, had a bitter primary battle in 1916 and were not fond of each other. With New out of office, Watson replaced Morgan with someone loyal to him, A.R. Harris.[382]

On July 1, 1930, the Prohibition unit was transferred from the Treasury Department to the Justice Department.[383] Then, in 1933, it was absorbed as a unit of the FBI. Hoover did not want to get involved in liquor enforcement because of the corruption that followed it. He downsized the unit by laying off more than eight hundred employees.[384] Shortly after the reorganization, Prohibition ended on December 5, 1933. What was left of the Prohibition bureau was transferred back to the Treasury Department. It eventually became the Bureau of Alcohol, Tobacco and Firearms (ATF). In addition to Anderson, the Prohibition unit lost four other agents in Indiana during its history.

FEDERAL NARCOTICS BUREAU

In the early 1900s, there was a major opium and cocaine epidemic in the United States. During the Civil War, soldiers were prescribed morphine for pain, leading to the first wave of opioid addiction. In 1898, Bayer marketed heroin as a solution to those suffering from morphine addiction. Free samples would be sent to morphine addicts, leading to heroin addiction. In the late 1800s, cocaine was endorsed for medicinal use, and tonics containing cocaine could be purchased in drugstores.[385] Popular products such as Coca-Cola contained cocaine, and in the Sears, Roebuck catalogue, one could buy a syringe with a small amount of cocaine for $1.50.[386]

America's growing drug addiction was blamed on physicians. They prescribed cocaine and morphine indiscriminately, creating thousands of new addicts each year. It was believed that 99 percent of addicts acquired their addiction from their physician. There was very little regulation at the state or federal level.[387] Indiana addressed the drug problem by passing the anti-cocaine law in 1913. The law strictly regulated the sale of morphine, opium, cocaine and heroin by physicians and pharmacists. The law provided for criminal fines and penalties under the administration of the state board of pharmacy.[388]

In 1914, the federal government passed the Harrison Narcotics Act, which required narcotics manufacturers, sellers and distributors to register with the Bureau of Internal Revenue (IRS). It was the first comprehensive law in the United States to regulate classes of drugs. The U.S. Treasury Department organized a narcotics bureau to pursue violators of the law. The federal government appointed Indianapolis pharmacist and head of the state pharmacy board Jerome J. Keene to oversee the enforcement of the law in Indiana.[389]

Prohibition also helped fuel America's drug addiction as people turned to drugs in the absence of alcohol. Until 1930, the Narcotics Bureau was a part of the Prohibition unit within the Department of the Treasury. The Porter Bill, named for Senator Stephen Porter of Pennsylvania, created a separate agency, the Federal Narcotics Bureau (FNB), within the Department of the Treasury. Harry J. Anslinger was selected as the first commissioner of the FNB, serving in the capacity for thirty-two years. The bill attempted to consolidate narcotic enforcement and effectively fight the war against illicit drugs.[390]

In the 1930s, a new drug, marijuana, became popular among high school students. Marijuana was believed to be an addictive drug that led people to commit murder and sexual assaults. Marijuana was not just smoked—it was also mixed with alcohol into a candy confection. People reported experiencing excitement and then a period of depression. Some reported becoming manic, and long-term use led to mental issues and violent episodes. Marijuana was commonly called "killer drug" and "crazy weed." Young people called the addicts "muggles." While the FNB was battling the smuggling of opium, cocaine and heroin into the country, marijuana was being grown in people's backyards, posing new challenges for the agency. In 1937, Congress passed the Marijuana Tax Act.[391]

In 1968, the FNB merged with the Bureau of Drug Abuse Control to form the Bureau of Narcotics and Dangerous Drugs (BNDD). Five years later, the BNDD merged to form the Drug Enforcement Agency (DEA).

During the FNB's existence, six agents were killed in the line of duty. The last agent killed was on December 19, 1967, in Gary, Indiana. Mansel Burrell was shot and killed while working an undercover heroin investigation. Burrell was seen leaving with a suspect in his vehicle, while another agent followed at a distance. The agent lost them in traffic. Fifteen minutes later, the agent found Burrell's vehicle parked outside an apartment building.

With no word from Burrell, they arrested the suspect last seen with him. The suspect finally confessed that his accomplice shot Burrell four times in the head before dumping his body in Illinois. Agent Burrell had been a federal agent for only fifteen months. At the age of twenty-three, he was the youngest federal officer to be killed in the line of duty at the time.[392]

CHAPTER 10

INDIANA STATE POLICE

Crime was rising across the country, more so in rural areas, and one of the main causes was the automobile. New and improved highways and new means of rapid transit combined to allow criminals to commit crimes and be miles away before law enforcement could be brought into action to apprehend them. Local law enforcement was ill-equipped to handle the problem, so states began considering needing a state police force. The idea of a state police force was not new, but it was also not popular.

Massachusetts created the first state police in 1865 to enforce alcohol, gambling and prostitution laws. It was abolished after ten years. Citizens preferred vigilante groups of private citizens rather than trusting a standing army to control crime. People distrusted a powerful central authority to tell them how to live their lives.[393] The animosity toward a state police force followed the same reasoning as why people favored states' rights over a centralized federal government. Citizens preferred local enforcement to that of a statewide police force.

Although Connecticut established a state police force in 1903 consisting of five officers to enforce alcohol and gaming violations,[394] it was Pennsylvania that set the model for other states when it created its state police force in 1905. The Pennsylvania State Police originated in the 1902 anthracite coal strike. A Pennsylvania law created the Coal and Iron Police, which allowed private companies to purchase police commissions for its officers. These officers, more than five thousand, existed to serve the interests of the mine owners. These officers would engage in unethical and criminal acts against the employees.[395]

The anthracite coal strike lasted from May 15 to October 23, causing a nationwide coal shortage. Governor William Stone called out the National Guard and President Theodore Roosevelt as a mediator to end the strike. Hearings into the cause of the strike recommended that peace and order be maintained by regularly appointed officers employed by the public. On May 2, 1905, Governor Samuel Pennypacker signed Senate Bill 278, creating the Pennsylvania State Police, the first uniformed police organization of its kind in the United States. Other states would follow their model in creating their own state police agencies.[396]

It took a brutal murder in New York to realize the benefits of a state police force. In 1912, four men shot Sam Howell, a construction foreman, seven times while he was delivering a sack of payroll money to his employees. Howell worked for the estate of Mrs. Moyca Newell in Bedford, a rural community in Westchester County. He was able to identify the four assailants before he died, but Newell could not get the sheriff to organize a posse to pursue the men. She launched a campaign, with the assistance of Katherine Mayo, author of *Justice to All: History of the Pennsylvania State Police*, to force New York to form a state police force. New York created its state police force in 1917 to provide protection to the state's rural areas. Subsequently, Newell was formally recognized in 1960 as the "Mother of the New York State Police."[397]

The idea of a state police force in Indiana was seriously considered after Michigan established its force in 1917, and other neighboring states were also considering it. There was concern that if other states established a state police force, Indiana would become fertile ground for criminals.[398] In 1919, the first proposal for a state police force in Indiana was made by Representative Demaree. The bill allocated $150,000 to the new organization. Mayors in more than a dozen cities opposed the idea of a state police force. Aside from the cost, there was concern that the state police would lower the morale of the various police organizations throughout the state. Police officers were opposed to the bill because of a fear that they would be embarrassed by the state police making petty arrests.[399] The bill was defeated in the House, never making it out of committee.[400]

While most farmers supported a state police force, it was met with opposition from organized labor. The Indiana State Federation of Labor opposed a state police force for fear that it would be used to break up strikes.[401] The Indianapolis streetcar strike of 1913 highlighted the fear of a state police force by organized labor. On October 31, streetcar workers went on strike in Indianapolis, causing a statewide disruption. On November 2, a riot broke out that lasted four days. The strike finally ended on November 7 with six people killed and more than one hundred injured.[402]

The strike helped Indiana get its first minimum wage law and a nine-hour workday, but it also showed glaring inadequacies with the local police department. Even after the Marion County sheriff had deputized 200 men to supplement the Indianapolis police, Mayor Shank and the chief of police admitted that they could not handle the situation. Governor Samuel Ralston called out the entire National Guard, 2,200 soldiers, and put the city under martial law.[403] During the strike, thirty-one Indianapolis police officers resigned when they refused to obey an order to ride on streetcars to protect strike breakers. They were willing to assist in keeping order, but they would not encourage strike breakers by protecting them.[404] The Board of Public Safety reinstated the officers over the objection of the chief of police and the board president, who had voted for conviction. They both resigned their positions after the vote was announced.[405] It also led to Indianapolis mayor Shank stepping down.[406]

In 1920, a crime wave swept the country in many major cities, including Indianapolis. Causes for the increased crime were blamed on liquor after the Eighteenth Amendment prohibiting alcohol in the United States went into effect nationwide on January 17, 1920. (Indiana outlawed alcohol two years earlier.) Other causes were lax enforcement of the laws, coddling of criminals and a higher cost of living.[407]

Indiana once again attempted to create a state police force that would protect the unprotected rural areas of the state and create a mobile force equipped with motorcycles and automobiles to catch criminals as they flee. State senator Arthur Baxter proposed a plan for 150 officers to work out of three locations at strategic points within the state. The officers would work with local police departments to preserve order and respond to calls for service in rural communities and assist motorists traveling the Indiana highways.[408]

Knowing that the bill would be hotly contested, Senator Baxter inserted provisions that would hopefully draw support and allay any fears of a state police force. In the event of a strike, the state police could not interfere unless life or property were in danger because of their inaction. If the strike was peaceful, they could only enter at the command of the superintendent or the governor.[409] This didn't satisfy organized labor. John L. Lewis, president of the United Mine Workers of America, said, "A benevolent despotism is the best form of government. It may be when it is benevolent, but it is the worst form when the despot is a tyrant and not benevolent."[410] The 1919

Gary steel strike was a recent example when the mayor of Gary called in the National Guard to enforce martial law against the strikers. By the next day, Gary was under federal control as the U.S. Army moved in to replace the National Guard.[411] There was not much trust between organized labor and government authorities.

The state police force was estimated to cost $300,000.[412] While some complained about the cost, supporters highlighted the cost of not having a state police force. The 1902 anthracite coal strike cost Pennsylvania $1 million by having nearly nine thousand National Guard troops on duty for more than one hundred days.[413] The 1913 Indianapolis streetcar strike cost the state $36,000 ($1,064,200 in 2023) for a strike that lasted only a week.[414] The benefits of a state police far outweighed the costs. In Michigan, 91 percent of arrests by state police officers resulted in a conviction—New York had 86 percent and Pennsylvania 90 percent. A state police force seemed to be a deterrent, as criminals avoided states where arrest and conviction were practically assured.[415]

Fear that the state police would become a political tool of the governor, Senator Baxter proposed that the state police be under the direct supervision of a superintendent appointed by the governor. The superintendent would lead for an indefinite amount of time. As a check and balance, the governor could not remove the superintendent except for incompetency, neglect of duty or malfeasance. Even then, the governor had to file a written statement, with the secretary of state stating the reasons for the removal.[416]

City mayors and police departments feared that untrained state police officers would be an embarrassment. Following the Pennsylvania model, officers selected for the state police would be army veterans. The officers would have to meet certain physical and mental requirements. The officers would be educated in the law and the rules of evidence to obtain a conviction.[417]

The state police bill took a hit when an alternative was introduced by Senator Oscar Ratts that proposed giving the county sheriffs more power. In an emergency, sheriffs could appoint as many deputies as they wanted. The deputies would be paid one dollar while serving, and the money would come from the general fund. At the time, deputies' salaries came from the sheriff's salary.[418] Critics of the sheriff bill emphasized the futility of the posse scheme of using untrained civilians to fight career criminals.[419] The sheriff-constable system used in the state's rural areas was viewed as a complete failure. As elected officials, they were not always the best people for the job but rather those who could garner the most votes. Deputies employed by the sheriff were mostly untrained, undisciplined and inefficient when handling emergency situations. Yet, these are the ones whom farmers must turn to for assistance.[420] The state police bill was defeated as the cost was prohibitive to many in the legislature.[421]

MOTOR VEHICLE POLICE

Although the Baxter bill was defeated, the desire for a state police force was not entirely over. A few months later, the Indiana legislature passed the Certificate of Title Act in 1921, which required motor vehicle owners to have a vehicle title issued by the secretary of state. The vehicle title doesn't have to be renewed unless the vehicle changes ownership. Under the new law, sheriffs and police officers must submit a list of stolen and recovered vehicles to the secretary of state. The secretary of state would send that list to every agency in the state.[422]

The purpose of the Certificate of Title Act was not so much to recover stolen vehicles but rather to keep thieves from stealing vehicles and disposing of them.[423] Since sheriffs and municipal police officers were limited to pursuing auto thieves, a state police force was needed to enforce the new law's provisions. Police powers were conferred on the secretary of state with the power to appoint deputies with statewide authority to recover stolen vehicles and apprehend auto thieves. Fees collected from motorists would go to fund the new unit, which was estimated to be nearly $350,000 for the first year.[424]

On June 1, 1921, Governor Warren McCray appointed Robert Humes as the first chief of the Indiana Motor Vehicle Police.[425] Secretary of State Ed Jackson and Humes appointed fifteen deputies, one from each Congressional district and two at large, to combat auto thefts across the state.[426] The officers used motorcycles to patrol the highways of Indiana in pursuit of auto thieves. The number of officers was well below the proposed 150,[427] but it set the groundwork for what eventually would become the Indiana State Police.

Although covering an entire state with such a small force seemed daunting, the motor vehicle police performed well. In the first six months, the unit recovered 118 vehicles and collected nearly $200,000 in registration fees.[428] In 1922, the first full year, the unit collected $250,000 in title and registration fees and recovered 200 vehicles.[429] While the motor police unit was profitable, it had limitations. It had no power to make arrests except in cases of registration violations or auto thefts.[430] It also never solved the problem of rural communities being vulnerable to criminals without adequate protection.

In 1923, Senator Robert L. Moorhead proposed a rural state police force consisting of eighty-four officers with full police powers to enforce any state crime. Because the motor vehicle police were so profitable, Moorhead proposed funding the unit with $300,000 from the auto theft fund. The rural police would cooperate with local police, sheriffs and private detective associations such as the Horse Thief Detective Association. It also called for the repeal of the 1921 act that gave sheriffs the authority to hire an unlimited number of deputies during times of emergencies.[431] After a contentious debate, the rural state police force bill was defeated, 32 to 14.[432] The rural communities had to continue to contend with the sheriff-constable system

The next proposal for a state police force came in 1925, this time at the urging of the Indiana Banker's Association. With six hundred of the eight hundred banks in the state located in rural towns, the situation was enticing for criminals.[433] Bankers in small towns favored a state police force, as the sheriff system proved inadequate. If a crime happened, the farmers' only option was to phone the nearest town, but it was too late by then. A farmer's crops were entitled to the same protection as a merchant's goods.[434]

The banking association proposed a police force of ninety-seven officers. The officers would serve an enlistment period of three years with a starting salary of $1,200 per year. The auto theft fund would entirely fund the new unit. The motor vehicle police numbered thirty-five officers and would be transferred to the new unit. A superintendent would head the rural police force, but unlike previous proposals, it would be controlled by a three-member commission. The governor would appoint the commissioners who would serve six-year terms without pay.[435] Even the state banking association wasn't enough to persuade the politicians to vote for the bill.[436] The banking association created its own statewide vigilante organization to assist in the capture of bank robbers.

The most that the legislature would agree to was granting the motor vehicle police the authority to enforce traffic laws. In 1924, 19,500 people were killed and more than 450,000 injured in motor vehicle crashes in the United States.[437] Indianapolis reported 70 deaths, giving it a higher death rate than New York City.[438] In 1925, the legislature passed the Automobile Regulation Act. Speed limits had increased to twenty-five miles per hour in the city and thirty-five miles per hour in the rural areas. Speeding was an arrestable offense and carried the suspension of driving privileges.[439]

Intoxicated driving was punishable as a felony.[440] The motor vehicle police could now enforce traffic laws, but criminal laws were still limited to auto thefts.

There was a grass-roots movement to establish a state police force in almost every state. A nonprofit organization, National Movement for State Police Inc., was formed to help organize and provide guidance for states as they established a state police force.[441] The organization began as the State Police Auxiliary Committee in 1919 to lobby state legislatures for the establishment of a state police force.[442] By 1927, state police agencies had been created in Connecticut (1903), Pennsylvania (1905), New York (1917), Michigan (1917), West Virginia (1919), Maryland (1921), New Jersey (1921), Maine (1921), Massachusetts (re-established in 1921), Utah (1923), Delaware (1923) and Rhode Island (1925). Bills had been introduced in the state legislatures in Indiana, Ohio, Illinois, Wisconsin, Minnesota and Missouri. The hope was that creating a nationwide movement for a state police force would put an end to criminals moving and jumping from one state to another.[443] The federal government was distrustful of southern states establishing state police for fear that it would be used to intimidate and oppress Black citizens.

In 1927, a major change came not only to the motor vehicle police but also to law enforcement across the state. At the insistence of automobile organizations, the legislature prohibited officers from making traffic stops unless the officers were wearing uniforms with a badge. Many state departments were unhappy with the new law, as it burdened the city with added costs. Marshals and constables normally wore plain clothes, as law enforcement was a side job to many. This change responded to a rise in police impersonators and organizations such as the Horse Thief Detective Association, whose members had constable powers. These individuals did not have the power to enforce traffic laws, and the unsuspecting motorist couldn't distinguish who was the legitimate authority.[444]

BUREAU OF CRIMINAL IDENTIFICATION AND INVESTIGATION

In the latter part of the nineteenth century, Alphonse Bertillon, a French criminologist and biometrics researcher, helped revolutionize law enforcement worldwide. He became dissatisfied with the recidivism rate in France, so he created a recordkeeping system that would allow police to identify recidivist criminals. To accurately identify criminals, the system took eleven measurements of certain body parts: height, head width, foot length, left middle finger, waist and the cubit (length of elbow to the middle finger). These were selected because they didn't change with weight gain. Distinctive characteristics such as eye color, hair color, deformities and scars were recorded. Bertillion also invented the mug shot, which included two photos, a face shot and a side profile. All of these items were recorded on a standardized index card that could be cross-indexed and easily retrieved.[445]

It became a popular tool in law enforcement. It was believed that no two people had the exact same measurements, and therefore each person had a unique place in the annals of criminology. The body parts that were measured never changed. A criminal may change his appearance or fool officers with a disguise, but they could not outsmart the Bertillion system.[446] The system was quickly adopted in the United States in most major cities. In 1896, the National Chiefs of Police Union founded the National Bureau of Criminal Identification as a national clearinghouse and resource for law enforcement.

In 1897, Indianapolis[447] and Evansville[448] were the first cities in Indiana to implement the Bertillion system. The first suspect to be subjected to the Bertillion system in Indianapolis occurred in 1898. Three rooms in the police department had been reserved for housing the Bertillion system under the command of John Engle. W.H. Lee, alias John Moran, was suspected of robbing a Washington, D.C. postmaster. His photo and measurements were taken, and he became the first person to be catalogued in the Bertillion system.[449] By 1915, Fort Wayne, Terre Haute, Lafayette, Gary, Michigan City, Columbus and Jeffersonville had all implemented the Bertillion system of identification.[450]

Around the same time that the Bertillion system was being implemented, another technological advancement in criminology was being used by the Argentine police: fingerprints. Juan Vucetich, an Argentine police official, devised the first workable fingerprint identification system. The first suspect to be convicted by fingerprint evidence was in 1892. The fingerprint system was offered as an alternative to the more complicated Bertillion system.[451] It became a valuable tool for law enforcement, as no two people, including identical twins, have the same fingerprints.[452]

In 1903, an incident at the federal penitentiary in Leavenworth, Kansas, highlighted the fallibility of the Bertillion system. In 1903, Will West was imprisoned after being convicted of manslaughter in Texas. He was photographed and measured per the Bertillion system. He was identified as a previous inmate who had committed murder by the prison clerk, but

West denied that he had ever been arrested. After pulling the index card for William West, the photograph and measurements on the card were identical to Will West. However, to the surprise of the prison staff, William West was already incarcerated at the prison. When the two inmates were brought together, they looked almost identical. However, a comparison of their fingerprints was not a match.[453] The West case showed that fingerprints were a better identification system than the Bertillion system. Although the West case was unique, most departments continued to use the Bertillion system but added fingerprint identification.

Although the State Banking Association was unsuccessful in establishing a state police force, all was not lost. It successfully lobbied the legislature to create the state bureau of criminal identification and investigation. This was seen as a major step toward creating a statewide police force. The motor vehicle police had already been organized into a separate bureau.[454] The law required that every sheriff fingerprint anyone convicted of a felony and submit the records to the bureau. While some departments already used the Bertillion and fingerprinting system, the bureau would act as a central depository. It was announced that within twelve hours of a person being fingerprinted, the bureau could locate the criminal record of the individual and determine if they were wanted by another agency or in another state.[455]

On July 1, 1927, the State Bureau of Criminal Identification and Investigation officially began operations. The unit was housed in room 417 at the Indiana Statehouse, which had previously been occupied by the recently abolished board of pardons.[456] There was a level of irony in the location. Secretary of State Frederick Schortemeier remarked, "The place where they let them out will soon be the room where they put them in."[457]

The new unit was placed in charge of Albert Perrott, head of the Bertillion system for the Indianapolis police. Two field agents would assist him: Forest H. Huntington, an operative with the Pinkerton Detective Agency, and Chauncey Manning, former chief of the detectives for the Indianapolis Police. The bureau required a good working relationship with police chiefs and sheriffs throughout the state. Oliver Wright, former police chief of Marion and former Grant County sheriff, would act as a liaison. Albert H. Schofield, an executive with the Monon and New York Central Railroads, would be the liaison with the state prison.[458]

THE CASE OF FRANK BADGLEY

It only took a few months before the Bureau of Criminal Identification showed how valuable of an asset it could be to the state. On Saturday, October 8, 1927, at 3:30 p.m., an individual robbed the Amboy State Bank in Miami County. The cashier, Paul Norris, and bookkeeper, Kathryn Lindley, were the only employees in the building. The robber stuffed $1,800 into a pillowcase, but his getaway was thwarted by a group of armed civilians.[459] In the absence of a state police force, the Indiana Banking Association had established a citizen vigilante organization that was imbued with police powers only during times of a bank robbery. In 1926, there were more than 1,600 vigilantes throughout Indiana.[460]

After the silent alarm was activated, nearly two hundred armed civilians surrounded the bank, including an off-duty Kokomo policeman, Clifton Small. The bank robber barricaded himself inside the bank. There was an exchange of gunfire, nearly thirty rounds, in which the cashier was shot in the leg. A bullet grazed the robber. He then grabbed Lindley and went outside, using her as a shield. The robber forced Lindley into his vehicle, but when she refused, he fled into a garage. Another exchange of gunfire commenced, but not before Officer Small was injured. The robber finally surrendered after tearing up all of the money.[461]

After his arrest, the suspect told the police that his name was Ray Arson and that he was from Detroit, Michigan. However, the Marion County sheriff recognized him as Frank Badgley of Indianapolis, who was wanted for a series of robberies. He told the authorities that he would die before revealing his true identity. But that wasn't needed, thanks to the Bureau of Criminal Identification. Fingerprints revealed his true identity to be twenty-nine-year-old Frank Badgley, with a criminal record dating back to when he was thirteen. His fingerprints linked him to numerous bank robberies, post office robberies and more than one hundred gas station robberies throughout Indiana. In cooperation with local agencies, the bureau was able to compile a complete criminal history of Badgley. His record was almost, if not longer, than that of Ralph Lee, the notorious criminal from Indiana.[462] His ability to break out of prison, more than thirteen times, gave him the nickname "Houdini."[463] Due to his extensive criminal history and the work by the bureau, he was charged as a habitual offender.[464]

Frank Badgley pleaded guilty and was sentenced to life in prison. The Indiana legislature passed a new law the previous year, giving judges discretion to give a life sentence for bank robbery (still a state crime) or auto theft. Badgley told the court at sentencing, "I was a bank robber because I wanted to be one. No one is to be blamed for my crimes. I failed, and now I am ready to accept my punishment."[465]

For all the work that the bureau did in convicting Badgley, he was paroled even after he attempted to break out of the Indiana State Prison with twelve other inmates in 1930. Some of those inmates were members of Dillinger's gang. In 1947, while on parole, Badgley and Robert Brown killed two Hammond police officers. Officer John J. Gerka was training a rookie officer, Donald Cook, as they investigated a suspicious vehicle. Upon approaching the vehicle, Gerka was shot in the chest with a .45-caliber pistol and died instantly. Cook, who had only been an officer for four days, was also shot and died two days later.[466] Badgley and Brown were found guilty of the murders and sentenced to death. They were executed in the electric chair on February 23, 1949. It was the third double execution in Indiana since the electric chair became the method of execution in the state in 1914.[467]

FORMATION OF THE INDIANA STATE POLICE

The election of 1928 ushered in a new wave of candidates into statewide office amid recent political scandals. Governor William McCray was forced to resign in 1924 and was later sentenced to ten years in federal prison for mail fraud. His governorship coincided with the rise of the Ku Klux Klan. After he resisted taking bribes from the Klan and vetoed Klan Day at the Indiana State Fair, he became a political target. McCray would rather go to jail than sacrifice his principles. For his refusal to assist the Klan, he was pardoned by President Herbert Hoover in 1930.[468] Governor Edward Jackson was indicted on bribery charges related to the Klan. The head of the Indiana Klan, D.C. Stephenson, was tried and sentenced to life for the murder of Madge Oberholtzer. Stephenson expected a pardon from Jackson, who helped to get him elected, but Jackson refused. Stephenson began revealing to reporters the number of politicians who had accepted bribes, including Jackson. He was tried, but it ended in a hung jury. The statute of limitations prevented him from being retried.[469]

With new state officeholders and legislators, there was a renewed attempt to establish a state police force. Newly elected state senator John L. Niblack from Marion County proposed a military-style system for the state police that would resemble the Royal Mounted Police in Canada. His bill called for an expansion of the motor vehicle police, two-year enlistment periods, desertion punishable as a misdemeanor, general arrest powers, for political affiliations to be kept private and officers to be housed in barracks strategically positioned throughout the state.[470] It also called for the establishment of three separate bureaus: clerical; criminal identification and investigation; and state police.[471]

In recent years, the motor vehicle police had become a political pawn. There was concern that the motor vehicle police gave the secretary of state too much power, as that position was seen as a steppingstone to the governorship. Some legislators advocated that the motor vehicle police should be placed within the governor's office. The previous secretary of state, Frederick E. Schortemeier, had attempted to use the motor vehicle police for personal reasons in his failed bid to become governor.[472] Senator Anderson Ketchum of Greensburg amended Niblack's bill to forbid the motor vehicle police from transporting voters to the polls. It didn't preclude officers from voting or taking part in elections but eliminated the use of state property to benefit or hinder a candidate's chance of election.[473]

Newly elected secretary of state Otto Fifield supported some parts of Niblack's bill. He was in favor of the expansion of the motor vehicle police from thirty to fifty men and modeling the police force after the military to eliminate politics within the agency.[474] He disagreed with giving the officers general arrest powers, as he preferred that they focus on traffic violations instead of criminal investigations. He preferred motorcycles to automobiles and believed that mounted patrol "was a costly experiment without merit." He also criticized the proposal of barracks from a social standpoint. Unmarried single men living in barracks lack the level of community attachment that married men who live at home in the community do.[475]

As in years past, bills establishing a state police force had always been controversial. Other legislators amended Niblack's bill, which soon hardly resembled the originally proposed bill. This was mostly attributed to a feud between Fifield and the newly elected governor, Harry Leslie. It began when Governor Leslie attempted to remove Marion County Republican boss George V. Coffin from his position. Coffin was involved with the Klan and was instrumental in getting Republican candidates elected. He had been indicted with ex-governor Jackson. Leslie disliked the Klan and disapproved of Coffin's methods. Leslie lost his battle with the Republican state committee to remove Coffin.[476] Governor Leslie was angered when Fifield would not lend his support in Coffin's ouster.[477]

After Niblack's bill sat dormant for a few weeks, it showed signs of life. This was attributed to Governor Leslie trying to wrestle control of the motor vehicle police from Fifield. Robert L. Moorhead, who authored a state police bill in 1923, amended Niblack's bill to merge the motor vehicle police and the Bureau of Criminal Identification and Investigation. The two bureaus would form a new department, the state department of public safety. The department would be controlled by a commission composed of the secretary of state, the board chairman and two members elected to four-year terms by the governor. Governor Leslie supported this, as it would separate the state police from the auto license department. It would also remove the motor vehicle police and the Bureau of Criminal Identification and Investigation from the individual control of the secretary of state.[478]

The opposition to the bill by organized labor had not changed. However, a new group, the automobile association, opposed the bill. They were against removing the motor vehicle police from the secretary of state's office. The office had all the vehicle records on file, and moving them to a new department would make it ineffective. They did support increasing the number of officers, as each officer, on average, was responsible for patrolling five counties.[479] Niblack's bill, like the others before it, was defeated. However, that didn't end the feud. A few months later, Governor Leslie's decision not to appoint Fifield to his crime commission was seen as a political move. It was another attempt to enlarge the power of the governor and reduce the power of the secretary of state.[480]

Ten months into Governor Harry Leslie's term, the country was thrust into the Great Depression. Like most other states, Indiana was dealing with increased crime. Governor Leslie formed a crime commission to investigate the causes, mostly from vice, narcotics and illegal liquor. The crime commission recommended a unified state system that could be efficiently mobilized against the criminal element. Republican senator C. Oliver Holmes and Democratic senator Thurman Gottschalk introduced a bipartisan proposal to combine the motor vehicle police and the bureau of criminal identification into a state department of public safety. Four members appointed by the governor would govern the new unit. It would remove the two departments from the secretary of state.[481]

The Great Depression was felt everywhere, and people needed someone to blame, and that was the Republicans. The election of 1930 ushered in a flurry of Democratic candidates. The bill creating the Board of Public Safety was defeated in the House, which had become overwhelmingly Democratic. The two departments would stay under the control of the secretary of state, which also had a new officeholder. Fifield lost his reelection as secretary of state and was replaced with Democrat Frank Mayr Jr. He was the first Democrat to hold the office since 1916, and the House ensured that he, not Governor Leslie, would retain control of the two bureaus.[482]

Mayr wasted no time in exerting his authority. He replaced Robert Humes, chief of the motor vehicle police, with Grover Garrett. He also terminated the entire police force. Forty-four officers were told not to report for duty. They were replaced with new officers.[483] The new force would be a "bone-dry" organization; if any officer was caught taking a drink, he would be immediately dismissed. The state police also got new uniforms. Forest-green shirts with black trousers and a black bowtie would separate the state police force from other police officers in the state and make them more easily identifiable.[484]

In 1932, more Republicans fell victim to the Depression as voters overwhelmingly replaced them with Democrats. Governor Leslie was replaced with Paul McNutt, and in the state legislature, Democrats claimed ninety-one of the one hundred seats in the House and forty-three out of the fifty seats in the Senate. Regardless of the political party, the state police continued to be a source of contention between the office of the governor and the secretary of state. Both political parties agreed that the state police had become a political tool of the secretary of state. Taxpayers were contributing $200,000 annually to fund the motor vehicle police, which the secretary of state used as his own political machine.[485]

People were done with the infighting over the state police. Bert Thurman, the Republican nominee for governor, advocated for the abolishment of the state police.[486] A special session of the legislature recommended the state police be brought under the control of the attorney general.[487] In 1932, another bipartisan attempt was made by Republican senators C. Oliver Holmes, J. Clyde Hoffman and John L. Niblack and Democrats Addison Drake and William V. Doogs. The proposal recommended merging the motor vehicle police, the Bureau of Criminal Identification, the fire marshal service and the oil inspectors into a state department of public safety. The board of safety would consist of the governor, secretary of state and attorney general, who would then appoint a director. The officers would have full police powers, and officers would not be dismissed because of their political affiliation.[488]

Finally, in 1933, the Indiana legislature passed the Executive Reorganization Act. On April 15, 1933, the Indiana State Police was officially created by law. It was immediately transferred from the secretary of state's office to the governor's office. The officers would have full police powers, not just be confined to enforcing traffic laws. The state police would be a part of the newly formed Department of Public Safety. Albert Feeney was appointed as the first director of the new department. That also made him the first superintendent of the newly formed Indiana State Police.[489]

Feeney wasted no time in reorganizing the new department. The position of chief was abolished and replaced with a captain to manage the day-to-day operations. Matt Leach of the Gary Police Department was selected to take over the new force. Half of the department was dismissed. A training school was established to compose a competent force devoid of politics.[490] He established a statewide radio system that would connect all sheriff and police departments with real-time information.[491] Despite all of this, Feeney was replaced in 1935 by Governor Paul McNutt for political reasons.

After nearly fifteen years of bickering over a state police force in Indiana, it got its first test as it went after Indiana's most notorious criminal, John Dillinger.

CHAPTER 11

PURSUIT OF DILLINGER

The newly formed Indiana State Police would soon be tested. Every available resource, including the federal government, would be needed to capture Indiana's most notorious criminal, John Dillinger. Born in Indianapolis, Dillinger was involved in petty crimes at a young age. In 1924, Dillinger was arrested for a robbery of a grocery store in Mooresville, Indiana, where he assaulted a customer. He was given a ten- to twenty-year sentence, serving time in the Indiana Reformatory in Pendleton and later the Indiana State Prison. On May 10, 1933, Dillinger was paroled, less than one month after the creation of the Indiana State Police.

Prison turned Dillinger into a hardened criminal. He was bitter about his lengthy prison sentence, and his wife, Beryl Hovious, divorced him while in prison. He was heartbroken, and with no home to go to after his release and the prospect of employment at rock bottom, he immediately turned to bank robbery. During his time in prison, he befriended veteran bank robbers Harry "Pete" Pierpont, Homer Van Meter and Charles Makley, among others. Dillinger implemented the Lamm system of robbing banks—named after Herman Lamm, who perfected the technique of "casing" a bank before robbing it.[492]

On July 21, 1933, Dillinger committed his first bank robbery at the New Carlisle National Bank in New Carlisle, Ohio. After entering the bank in the middle of the night, Dillinger and two others lay in wait until the bank opened in the morning. Surprising the bank employees, Dillinger made off with $10,000.[493] A series of robberies followed: July 17, the Commercial Bank in Daleville, Indiana, of $3,500; August 4, the Montpelier National Bank in

Montpelier, Indiana, of $12,000;[494] August 14, Bluffton Bank in Bluffton, Ohio, of $2,000; and Massachusetts Avenue State Bank in Indianapolis, of $24,800. At this time, Captain Leach of the Indiana State Police labeled Dillinger "Indiana's public enemy No. 1."[495]

On September 22, S.E. Yendes, chief of detectives with the Dayton police, was alerted that Dillinger was staying at a home on West First Street. Shortly around 1:00 a.m., a group of officers armed with shotguns, rifles and guns wearing bulletproof vests raided the house. It happened so quickly that Dillinger had no time to react. In his possession, officers found four pistols, rifle cartridges and shotgun shells, $2,600 and notes detailing the quickest routes out of various cities, including Michigan City, Indiana. Coincidentally, that is where the Indiana State Prison is located. Sacks of carpet tacks were recovered, which was important because tacks were used to throw across the roads to puncture tires.[496]

While in Dayton, he was under constant guard, with officers positioned outside his cell and more officers perched above it in case of an attempted escape. Dillinger was wanted in connection with multiple robberies in different cities. Although the local authorities allowed detectives to interview Dillinger, the decision was made to try him in Ohio for the Bluffton bank robbery. He was transferred to the Allen County Jail in Lima. They left nothing to chance. Two Dayton police cars with officers armed with shotguns and rifles escorted Dillinger to Piqua, Ohio, and facilitated the exchange with Allen County sheriff Jess Sarber. From Piqua, two Lima police vehicles escorted the sheriff's vehicle to the jail.[497]

Four days after Dillinger's capture in Dayton, a spectacular prison break occurred at the Indiana State Prison. Ten inmates escaped from the prison, including some of Dillinger's friends, Russell Clark, Walter Dietrich, Harry Pierpont and Charles Makley. The escape began in the shirt factory when the assistant warden was summoned due to an equipment malfunction. Seven inmates armed with pistols and three with clubs surprised the warden. Along with the plant superintendent, they were forced to follow the inmates through a ventilation tunnel that led back into the cell block. Each inmate carried a bundle of shirts that concealed the handguns. As they appeared to be taking the shirts back to the factory and being escorted by the warden and superintendent, the guards didn't question it. The warden was unable to notify the prison guards. As they neared the front gate, they stormed the prison clerk's office looking for weapons and money. The prison clerk, Finley P. Carson, was shot by the inmates. They fled when the prison alarm finally sounded.

Once outside the prison, they encountered Harrison County sheriff Charles Heel, who had dropped off prisoners from Corydon. Three inmates overpowered the sheriff, taking his weapon and commandeering his vehicle, as well as taking him with them. The other seven inmates stole a car belonging to two women. The sheriff's vehicle was eventually abandoned near Wheeler, Indiana. They stole a local farmer's vehicle, which was later found near Valparaiso. It appeared that the inmates were heading to Chicago.[498] Sheriff Heel was later found unharmed.

It is believed that Dillinger was the mastermind behind the prison escape. He was able to smuggle weapons into the shirt factory successfully. The Indiana State Police had their first real test, which was daunting. They did not have the manpower for something this big, and they were forced to call out three companies of the Indiana National Guard to assist.[499] The finger-pointing for blame began almost immediately. Sixty-nine experienced prison guards had been recently replaced with untrained guards due to political patronage.[500] Leach accused the Dayton police of not sharing information. Dillinger was found with a map of the prison and escape routes, and that information was never handed over to the Indiana State Police when they came to Dayton to question him.[501]

The escaped convicts, along with a few others, formed the Dillinger Gang, also referred to as the Terror Gang. Their first bank robbery as an organized gang was the First National Bank in St. Marys, Ohio, of $15,000 on October 3. The money was to be used to free Dillinger, still housed in the Allen County Jail.[502] On October 12, Pierpont, Makley, Clark and Harry Copeland, a parolee, posed as Indiana State Police officers. They told Sheriff Sarber that they were there to extradite Dillinger back to Indiana. Sarber seemed to recognize Copeland, and he asked for their identification. The bandits pulled out their pistols. As the sheriff reached for his pistol, he was shot in the abdomen. Hearing the gunfire, Sarber's wife and Deputy Wilbert Sharpe responded and were immediately seized and locked in a cell. Sarber was transported to a hospital but later died of his injuries. He was able to identify Copeland as one of the assailants, while Pierpont was identified as the shooter.[503]

With Dillinger freed, the gang focused on acquiring weapons and equipment. There was no better place than robbing the police departments. On October 15, three members stormed the Auburn, Indiana police station, overcoming the two officers on duty. They escaped with a machine gun, seven rifles, several pistols and three bulletproof vests.[504] On October 21, the gang raided the Peru, Indiana police department. They made off with more weapons and bulletproof vests, as well as tear gas guns and three police badges.[505] Fully equipped with weapons, the gang robbed the Central National Bank in Greencastle of $75,000 on October 23, and the next day, they robbed the Western State Bank in South Bend of $5,000.[506]

Dillinger's gang had become nearly unstoppable. Every available resource was used to bring this lawless gang of desperados to justice. Governor McNutt increased the state police from fifty-eight to ninety-two officers, one officer for each county. The National Guard had been put on standby. The American Legion mobilized its members to form a "shotgun army" to blockade roads and assist law enforcement. Citizen vigilance committees sprang into action. Although the Dillinger Gang had not committed a federal crime, McNutt requested the assistance of federal agents.[507]

Authorities came close to capturing Dillinger on November 16 in Chicago. Working on a tip, sixteen Indiana state police officers and three squads of Chicago police officers waited as Dillinger's vehicle stopped in front of a doctor's office. However, when Dillinger left, he took a different route than expected. A police chase ensued, with shots being fired. Dillinger had a woman with him, and they both took turns firing at the police. The police had to give up the chase, as the officer's bullets proved to be ineffective against the bulletproof windows Dillinger had installed.[508]

On November 20, the Dillinger Gang robbed the American Bank and Trust in Racine, Wisconsin, of $27,000. During the robbery, the gang wounded the cashier and police sergeant Wilbur Hansen. To avoid a shootout with the police, they took three hostages, using them as shields. Once they were safely away, they released the hostages, which included the bank president, bookkeeper and Racine police officer Cyril Boyard.[509] At the same time of the robbery, an intoxicated Copeland was captured in Chicago. He was escorted across the state line, where he was taken back to the Indiana State Prison.[510]

Authorities in Indiana and Ohio mostly pursued Dillinger's gang, but that changed when the gang moved its headquarters to Chicago. On December 14, Sergeant William Shanley, a twenty-year veteran, was killed by John "Red" Hamilton as he attempted to arrest him. The Chicago police formed the "Dillinger Squad" with orders to shoot and kill any members of the group.[511]

EUGENE TEAGUE

While Dillinger and his girlfriend, Evelyn Frechette, were in Daytona Beach, Edward Shouse, a member of the Dillinger Gang and escapee from the state prison, was in Paris, Illinois. The Indiana State Police received a tip that Shouse would be meeting someone in front of the LaFrance hotel to rob a bank in the city. The state police, under Leach's command, was cooperating with the authorities in Paris. Shouse's vehicle pulled up in front of the hotel at 11:00 a.m. with two female companions.

After the Dillinger Gang killed Sheriff Sarber and Chicago sergeant Shanley, Leach was not about to take any chances. He ordered Trooper Teague to ram Shouse's vehicle. Leach had also given orders to shoot and kill. Lieutenant Chester Butler, Teague's superior officer, had been posted in a sharpshooter position on the hotel steps. After Teague rammed the vehicle, the officers were to open fire. It isn't known if Teague had been fully briefed on the operation, but he jumped out of his vehicle and ran to Shouse's driver's door to pull him out. That put him in the line of fire as the shots rang out. While the two women escaped unharmed, Teague was shot, and Shouse easily surrendered.

Teague died a few hours later at a Paris hospital. Butler was clearly distraught and heartbroken over the death of Teague. He was his supervisor as well as his friend. He accepted all responsibility, but Leach said that it was an unfortunate accident and that no one was to blame. Teague, who had been a state police officer since May, shortly after the force was established, became the first officer in the agency's history to die in the line of duty. Shouse was immediately taken back to the Indiana State Prison.[512]

EAST CHICAGO BANK ROBBERY

After Dillinger's Florida vacation, he returned to Indiana to rob the First National Bank in East Chicago on January 15, 1934. He committed the bank robbery with John Hamilton, who was responsible for killing Chicago officer Shanley. They entered the bank at 2:50 p.m., ten minutes before closing. Hamilton was already waiting inside as Dillinger walked in carrying a briefcase. Dillinger pulled out a Thompson submachine gun, and they immediately went to work. Unknown to Hamilton or Dillinger, the bank's vice-president signaled the silent alarm.

While they were inside, eight East Chicago police officers surrounded the bank, apparently oblivious that the getaway car was still parked outside. After securing $20,000, Hamilton and Dillinger took two bank employees as shields to avoid being shot by the police. As they made their way to the getaway car, Officer William Patrick O'Malley was just a few feet away from Dillinger. O'Malley fired four shots at Dillinger, but they had no effect, as he wore a bulletproof vest. Dillinger pushed his hostage out of the way and fired eight rounds quickly, killing O'Malley instantly. The two hostages escaped while Hamilton and Dillinger fled in their vehicle. Hamilton was wounded in the hand, causing him to lose his weapon. Two state game wardens gave chase, but they were no match, and they got away. The death of O'Malley was the first and only murder directly attributed to Dillinger.[513]

CAPTURE IN ARIZONA

With so many agencies pursuing the Dillinger Gang, they left the Midwest to lay low. They headed west, ending up in Tucson, Arizona, living a life of luxury in the upscale Congress Hotel. On the night of January 21, a fire broke out in the hotel's dining room. The guests were forced to evacuate while the fire department extinguished the flames. One of the firefighters recognized the gang members from pictures circulating in the true crime magazine *True Detective*. They offered $50 to a firefighter to retrieve their luggage from the burned-out building. Once the police became aware, they were put under surveillance; they were discovered to be renting a house in an exclusive neighborhood. On January 25, the police closed in and arrested Dillinger, Makley, Pierpont, Clark and their girlfriends without firing a single shot. In their possession, the police recovered five machine guns, pistols, 3,500 rounds of ammunition, $40,000 and $12,000 in diamonds.[514]

The Dillinger Gang was under heavy guard by fifty officers surrounding the Pima County Jail. Upon hearing of the arrest, Leach and four officers traveled to Tucson to bring Dillinger back to Indiana to stand trial for the murder of Patrolman O'Malley. There was a race to Tucson as six different states wanted to extradite Dillinger. Dillinger wanted to be extradited back to Wisconsin, where they didn't have the death penalty. Arizona governor B.B. Mouer assured Indiana authorities that Dillinger would be extradited back to them, but the others would go to Ohio to stand trial for the murder of Sheriff Sarber.[515] Dillinger was brought back to Indiana by an American Airways plane landing at Chicago's Midway Airport. Makley, Pierpont and Clark traveled to Ohio by private train.[516]

Although Captain Leach preferred that Dillinger be housed in the state prison, Lake County sheriff Lillian Holley proclaimed that the county jail was impenetrable with a staff of well-trained officers.[517] However, on March 3, Dillinger escaped from the Lake County Jail using a pistol he carved out of wood. He escaped from the jail with a Black prisoner, Herbert Youngblood, awaiting trial for first-degree murder. They took Deputy Ernest Blunk hostage, forcing him to drive them to Illinois. They got away in a 1933 Ford V-8 that belonged to Sheriff Holley.[518] The federal government was assisting in Dillinger's apprehension at the local authorities' request. However, the theft of the sheriff's car became a federal crime, as he violated the Dyer Act prohibiting the transportation of stolen vehicles across state lines.[519]

After his escape, Dillinger's gang, except for Hamilton, had either been captured or killed. With Hamilton, they created a second gang by merging with Baby Face Nelson's gang, which included Homer Van Meter, Tommy Carroll and Eddie Green. They were responsible for robbing the Securities National Bank and Trust in Sioux Falls, South Dakota, of $49,500;[520] the First National Bank in Mason City, Iowa, of $52,000 on March 13;[521] and the First National Bank in Fostoria, Ohio, of $17,000 on May 3.[522]

The Dillinger Gang's last bank robbery was on June 30 in South Bend, Indiana. The gang entered the Merchants National Bank, making off with $20,000 in the most violent robbery to date. Four people were seriously injured when the bandits opened fire. Van Meter waited outside and took a position at the corner of Wayne and Michigan Streets. Officer Howard Wagner was directing traffic at the same location. When he noticed Van Meter, he opened fire. Van Meter was quicker and struck Officer Wagner with a hail of bullets. As the gang fled the scene, Detective Harry Henderson opened fire on the vehicle, striking Van Meter.[523] They would eventually assault a local doctor, Leslie Laird, forcing him to provide medical attention to Van Meter.[524]

After Dillinger broke out of the Lake County Jail, J. Edgar Hoover labeled Dillinger as "Public Enemy No. 1." He formed a task force to capture Dillinger under the command of Samuel Cowley and the assistance of Melvin Purvis, agent in charge of the Chicago field office. The task force headquarters was based out of Chicago. While the Indiana State Police welcomed federal assistance, it wanted Dillinger to answer for the murder of O'Malley and Wagner. On July 22, 1934, Dillinger's luck ran out. Federal agents shot and killed Dillinger as he was leaving the Biograph Theater in Chicago.[525]

Dillinger's gang was responsible for the deaths of thirteen law enforcement officers. Stopping Dillinger required cooperation among the federal government, state police, local police and the assistance of citizen groups. This was a time when the different agencies insisted on autonomy, but they realized that a single agency or group could not do it alone.

GALLERY 2

Top: A group of bank vigilantes in Iowa. The Iowa Plan became a template for other states to establish their own vigilante groups. *Darcy Maulsby*.

Bottom: Suspected draft dodgers picked up in a "slacker raid" in New York City, 1918. The AFL targeted draft dodgers around the country. *Library of Congress*.

CHARLES J. ORBISON,
Federal Prohibition Director for Indiana.

Left: Charles Orbison, first Prohibition director in Indiana. *From the* Indiana Daily Times, *January 12, 1921.*

Below: Officers of the Indiana State Police motorcycle unit. *Indiana State Police Museum.*

Opposite, top: Indiana State Police officer sitting on his 1931 Harley-Davidson VL. *Indiana State Police Museum.*

Opposite, bottom: Group of civilians gathering to defend themselves. *From the* Star Press, *August 15, 1937.*

Top: Second annual shootout of the Indiana Banker Vigilantes at Fort Benjamin Harrison. *Lake City Bank*.

Bottom: Indianapolis police, 1874. *Indianapolis Public Library*.

THE HOOSIER BANKER

Officially Representing

INDIANA BANKERS ASSOCIATION

VOL. XII No. 9 INDIANAPOLIS, IND., JUNE, 1927 SINGLE COPY, 25c

Muncie Bank Women Firing on the Pistol Range in the Basement of the Bank

Women were recruited as vigilantes to fight against bank robbers. *Lake City Bank.*

Left: Governor Oliver Morton, Indiana's Civil War governor, served from 1861 to 1867. *Public domain image.*

Right: Frank Reno, a member of the Reno Gang, carried out the first peacetime train robbery in the United States. He was one of four taken from the jail and lynched by a mob. *Indiana State Library.*

This flag announcing that "a man was lynched yesterday" was flown from the upper-story window of the NAACP headquarters at 69 Fifth Avenue, New York City. *Library of Congress.*

Wanted poster for John Dillinger, Baby Face Nelson and Pretty Boy Floyd. *Indiana State Police Museum.*

Charles Mackey and Marion County sheriff Otto Ray pose with a submachine gun next to new Buick patrol cars. *Patrick Pearsey.*

Indianapolis police in 1916. *Patrick Pearsey*.

A badge worn by members of the Horse Thief Detective Association. *National Horse Thief Detective Association Collection, Robert T. Ramsay Jr. Archival Center, Lilly Library, Wabash College, Crawfordsville, Indiana.*

On July 30, 1916, German agents blew up the Black Tom railroad yard. The explosion destroyed 2 million tons of war materials. *Public domain image.*

Bernard Goetz, "Subway Vigilante," opened fire on four Black men on the New York City subway on December 22, 1984. *From the* New York Post.

PROTECTION FOR BANKS

Riot Guns, Rifles, Revolvers, Automatic Pistols

We can supply you with any kind of guns you desire, and can give you a price that is *right.* Many banks are buying guns for inside and outside use.

Write for full information and prices.

611 Indiana Trust Building
Indianapolis

Advertisement for weapons to be supplied to banks for protection. *Lake City Bank.*

A fire broke out at the Hotel Congress in Tucson, Arizona, where Dillinger was staying. He was arrested and transported back to Indiana, later escaping. *From the* Arizona Daily Star, *January 24, 1934.*

Children standing in front of an anti-German sign in Edison Park, Chicago, 1917. *Library of Congress.*

The Reno Gang, with brothers John, Frank, Simeon and William. *Public domain image.*

Above: Graves of the Reno brothers in Seymour, Indiana. *Author photo.*

GOVERNOR ED JACKSON.

Right: Edward Jackson, governor of Indiana from 1925 to 1929. *From the* Indianapolis Star, *September 10, 1927.*

CHAPTER 12

GUARDIAN ANGELS

During the 1970s, the crime rate in New York City reached historic levels, so much so that the city became known as "Fear City." A few factors led to the increase. NYPD officer Frank Serpico exposed widespread corruption within the police department, which led to the Knapp Commission's final report on reforms in 1972. Many attributed police corruption to rising crime. "It is senseless to believe youngsters do not see this or to expect that it will create in them a respect for the law," said Manhattan Borough president Percy Sutton.

New York City was in severe financial trouble. The city had filed for bankruptcy with the State Supreme Court to avoid defaulting on $100 million in loans. Bankruptcy was avoided when the city agreed to deep budget cuts. In 1975, the city laid off fifteen thousand workers, including thousands of cops and firefighters. The NYPD was forced to end overnight subway patrols to focus on more daytime crime.[526]

Son of Sam killer David Berkowitz began terrorizing the city in 1977. That summer was characterized by blackouts, looting and fires, costing the city more than $300 million in property damage and leading to 3,700 arrests. It became so bad that a survival guide was created for visitors. The four-page pamphlet urged visitors not to visit, but if they should, there was a list of rules that should be followed: staying off the street after 6:00 p.m., not walking anywhere, avoiding public transportation and remaining in Manhattan. It made New York City sound more like a war zone than an American city.[527]

New York City was in turmoil, and a reduced police force was struggling to deal with rising crime. The subway became one of the most dangerous places in the city. Curtis "Rock" Sliwa, a twenty-three-year-old McDonald's manager from the South Bronx, was tired of the criminal element and decided to stand up to the muggers, drug dealers and thieves terrorizing the citizens. He recruited twelve other like-minded people to patrol and combat crime on the subway.

Originally known as the Magnificent 13, the group was active in making citizen arrests and helping the police apprehend criminals. The members' distinctive red berets, black boots and white T-shirts with red lettering were easily recognizable. While many residents were happy to see their presence, there were just as many skeptics. Mayor Ed Koch referred to them as "vigilantes in sneakers."[528]

Being a crime crusader did come with dangers. In April 1979, the Magnificent 13 were patrolling the Brooklyn-bound trains when they noticed six individuals circling a woman with malicious intentions. Sliwa and two companions jumped into action. The group had some basic martial arts training. Sliwa landed a flying kick on a six-foot-six assailant carrying a shotgun. His kick made contact with the assailant's head, but his momentum carried him off the platform, where he fell seventeen feet to the ground. It was described as something out of a kung fu movie. The would-be rapists scurried off, and the Magnificent 13 won the battle. It came with a cost, as Sliwa suffered severe back and leg injuries. The encounter made politicians take a second look at the group. Lieutenant Governor Mario Cuomo looked into getting the group insurance coverage, and the New York legislature gave the group a standing ovation.[529]

The group grew to thirty-eight young men and women. A few months after the subway incident, the group introduced a new name, the Guardian Angels. In addition to the red beret, they wore black Turkish-style pants, white T-shirts emblazoned with the Guardian Angels logo and red sashes. Their uniform pays homage to Shaolin kung fu, one of the oldest and largest martial arts styles.[530]

The group started expanding out of the subway and into the parks and other modes of transportation. Central Park had become one of the most dangerous areas in New York City at night. Some group members patrolled the park in uniform, while others went undercover, posing as joggers, lovers and vagrants. They protected the park against muggers, armed robbers and rapists. The NYPD and the Parks Department expressed skepticism of the group's efforts, and the operation smacked of vigilantism.[531]

By October 1979, the group had grown to 162 members and further expanded its operations to buses in Brooklyn. The buses had become a haven for Jesse James–type robberies. Although there was a need to protect the citizens, there was a more personal reason. Many relatives of the Guardian Angels were victims, which necessitated their involvement. The NYPD and the Transit Police still did not recognize the group because they were concerned about their safety. Eighteen-year-olds were no match for armed criminals. However, there were still organizations and state leaders that applauded their efforts.[532]

In just a few short years, membership had grown to seven hundred. The group accepted people from all races, but it was mostly made up of Black and Hispanic residents from the lower-income areas of New York. The youths ranged from reformed gang members and high school dropouts to college graduates. With the increased membership, a better organizational structure was needed.

The city was divided into sections, with each having its own chapter. Each chapter had a commander who was answerable to Sliwa. There were no solo patrols, and each member had to follow a strict code of conduct. Weapons were not allowed to be carried, and members searched one another before they went on patrol. They had to pay their own bus or subway fares, and minor offenses, such as smoking on the subway, were grounds for expulsion.[533]

The Guardian Angels came at a time when not only citizens needed them but also many of the disenfranchised youth themselves. They were looking for a place to belong, which was the same reason gang membership was rising. One of the biggest supporters of the Guardian Angels was the Bronx district attorney Mario Merola. He remarked, "They are searching for a cause, there's a big void in their lives, and this is the way some of them fill it." Instead of joining gangs, they were doing something good for their community.

Sliwa was credited with motivating youths where traditional institutions, such as church and school, had failed. While most Guardian Angels came from poor backgrounds, Sliwa would not let anyone use poverty or living conditions as an excuse for crime. He wanted the Guardian Angels to become role models for other youths. It didn't take long before chapters began to form outside New York City.[534]

By 1981, the Guardian Angels membership had grown to 2,235 youths in twenty different chapters across the country. Youths as young as sixteen could join in the effort to rid their community of crime. Sliwa had introduced a selection process that included supplying three references, passing a physical fitness test and undergoing a three-month training program. Future Guardian Angels learned about the legal system, citizen's arrest and martial arts.[535]

In many cities, Guardian Angels were a welcome addition in the fight against crime. Los Angeles was the first West Coast city to get a chapter. A spokesman for the LAPD remarked, "We look to the Guardian Angels as an extension of our neighborhood watch groups." New Orleans welcomed the Guardian Angels and even paid for Sliwa to come there and set up a chapter.

But not every city was friendly to the Guardian Angels, and they continued to be viewed as vigilantes. Sliwa rejected that idea and argued that the Guardian Angels were role models. "We're trying to revive an old tradition of 40, 50 years ago, when people would actively and physically intervene when they saw a crime go down. People don't do that anymore, and we are showing that they can," according to Sliwa. The police and mayors of major cities viewed Guardian Angels as a law enforcement problem.

When Sliwa showed up in Chicago, the mayor, Jane Bryne, told him to "go fly a kite," while the police referred to them as a "goon squad." In Detroit, they were called "turkeys" and "jerks," and they were threatened with arrest in Cleveland.[536] Sometimes the reception turned physical, as when Sliwa was thrown into the Potomac River while trying to set up a chapter in Washington, D.C. Sliwa claimed that his assailants were police officers.[537]

Sliwa knew that what they were doing was dangerous. As foreshadowing, Sliwa, was quoted as saying that "there may be casualties, and we know this and are willing to accept that time when someone may pull out a gun and blow our brains out."[538] In December 1981 came the first Guardian Angel fatality when Frank Melvin was killed while on patrol in Newark, New Jersey. However, the killer was not a career criminal but rather a police officer, in a case of mistaken identity.

GUARDIAN ANGELS ARRIVE IN INDIANA

By 1983, the Guardian Angels had forty-three chapters across the United States and three in Canada. Sliwa had his eyes on Indiana for an expansion into four cities. Gary was the first city to welcome the Guardian Angels. A city of 170,000 people, it was experiencing a 17.3 percent unemployment rate and a high crime rate. Of the five largest cities in Indiana, it had the highest number of murders at ninety-one, an increase of six from the previous year.

The arrival of the Guardian Angels coincided with an election year. The mayor of Gary, Richard Hatcher, was the first Black mayor of a large American city. First elected in 1967, he was pursuing a fifth term in 1983. For the first time, he had a legitimate primary challenger, city council member Thomas Crump. The rising crime rate became a vocal point of the campaign. While the overall crime rate had decreased in 1982, murders, auto theft and arson had increased. Burned-out houses dotted the city because of busted fire hoses and lack of water pressure. Senior citizens were afraid to go outside even during the day.[539]

While the campaign wore on, the Gary police were at odds with one another. A group of policemen condemned the mayor and Chief of Police Frederick Kowsky's public safety record. They argued that there were manpower shortages, inadequate equipment and poor morale within the department. Another set of officers formed a group called Policemen for a Positive Gary to refute those allegations.[540] The campaign exposed major issues with the quality of life in Gary.

Residents of the Glen Park neighborhood invited the Guardian Angels to Gary over concerns about the rising crime rate.[541] Mayor Hatcher welcomed the youth crime fighters with open arms. He provided training lectures from the Gary Police Department Community Affairs officers and provided space for the Guardian Angels to train.[542] According to Sliwa, their arrival in Gary was "the best reception I've ever had. Period."[543] Whether it was sincere or a political move, it worked, as Hatcher won the primary.

But not everyone was receptive to their arrival. Chief of Police Kowsky, who was a former NYPD officer, was openly opposed to the Guardian Angels.[544] After a ten-week training period, the Guardian Angels performed their first patrol on July 28, 1983. It was an extremely hot day, and two girls on patrol passed out from heat exhaustion. A city bus driver who opposed the Guardian Angels' philosophy of people helping other people refused to help the two girls. Even though he had an empty air-conditioned bus, he would let the girls die if they didn't have the sixty cents for the fare. He eventually did call an ambulance, and the girls were treated at an area hospital.[545] This was just another example of the type of resistance the Guardian Angels had to contend with, whether it was from politicians, government officials or citizens.

Sliwa had plans to set up chapters in nearby Hammond and East Chicago, but the welcome was cold and uninviting. He got the cold shoulder when he met with Hammond mayor Edward J. Raskosky, who feared that the Guardian Angels would promote a form of violent street justice; his meeting with Sliwa lasted only minutes. Sliwa was quoted as saying that Mayor Raskosky "treated me like a dog who had fleas."[546] It didn't get any better after Sliwa showed up at city hall and interrupted a private meeting flanked by television cameras and reporters.[547]

Being unwelcome guests did not deter the Guardian Angels from establishing chapters in Hammond and East Chicago. They just didn't enjoy the public support that Gary showed them. The first class of twenty graduates in Hammond took to the streets in October 1983,[548] while a small three-person unit patrolled East Chicago.[549]

The Guardian Angels' arrival in Indianapolis was met with the same opposition. The city objected to them because they were a poorly trained vigilante group that only answered to other Angels. A police force draws its authority from the citizens of the community, while Angels draw their authority from only themselves.[550] Some viewed the Guardian Angels as a future law and order coalition that could become a power base for raising funds and wielding political influence. In 1982, the organization had raised $72,000, and there was suspicion of politics at play when the Angels came to Gary.[551]

Indianapolis became the fiftieth chapter of the organization, and 250 people showed up for the selection process to become Angels. High-quality recruits and a wide support base among the community made Indianapolis a model city for future chapters.[552] The city refused to give the Guardian Angels an agreement, mostly because of liability issues. Instead, the community relations division of the Indianapolis Police Department was named as a liaison with the Angels.[553]

There were times when the Guardian Angels proved their worth. The Angels broke up a theft at Circle City in Indianapolis,[554] and they patrolled around the clock at the Columbia Center, a public housing project in Hammond, after a seventy-seven-year-old woman was brutally raped.[555] But a series of public relations disasters tarnished the reputation of the Angels.

When the Guardian Angels arrived in Gary, Sliwa gave most of the credit to the chapter's leader, Joe DeMarti. Born and raised in Lake County, he led the effort to get a chapter in Gary. He spent $2,000 of his own money to print flyers and went door to door to recruit members. Gary was the first city to roll out the red carpet for the Guardian Angels. DeMarti went to Joliet, Illinois, to assist law enforcement with seventeen unsolved murders in a two-month period. He was recognized nationally for his efforts. Sliwa referred to him as the "archangel" of Gary.[556]

But DeMarti was living a double life. While organizing a Guardian Angels chapter to fight crime in his neighborhood, he secretly sold automatic weapons. He was captured after a sixteen-month investigation by the Bureau of Alcohol, Tobacco and Firearms that began in 1982. During the course of the investigation, undercover agents bought nearly 150 weapons ranging from machine guns to pistols and sawed-off shotguns, as well as silencers. Some of those weapons were reported stolen from local police departments. Six other individuals were also arrested, including a former Gary police officer.[557]

As a result of the investigation, the Lake County sheriff, Rudy Bartolomei, became the focus of a federal probe. Some of the weapons sold to federal agents were once kept in the property room at the sheriff's department and somehow found their way back onto the street. He was already under investigation by the FBI for misuse of public money during his time as county commissioner.[558] In 1985, he was indicted on corruption charges.[559] DeMarti pleaded guilty to one count of an illegal kit capable of turning a high-powered rifle into a machine gun and received three years. In exchange, they agreed to drop the five counts of illegal possession and unlawful sale of firearms, which carried a sentence of ten years.[560]

While DeMarti was accepting a plea deal, two other Angels from the Gary chapter were arrested for the kidnapping, rape, robbery and attempted murder of a Merrillville woman. The two members, Jerome Henderson and Richard Perez, and a nonmember, William Baker, kidnapped a woman from the Zayre parking lot in Merrillville on August 23, 1983. They robbed her and drove her around town for several hours. They took her to a wooded area near the Grand Calumet River. After they raped her, she was bound, gagged and thrown into the river. They fired three shots at her while she floated down the river. She survived, and the two Guardian Angels were arrested. Henderson, who led the attack, got fifty years in prison, while Baker got forty years.[561] Perez testified against the other two and received a twenty-year sentence. The defense claimed that Perez falsely accused them because he was upset at being suspended by the Guardian Angels.[562]

The image of the Guardian Angels was severely damaged. The Gary and Hammond chapters were left with no leadership, and Sliwa put those chapters under the control of the Chicago chapter. All members were subjected to additional background checks. Four members were dismissed from the Gary chapter in a shakeup of the organization. It was determined that although they had no personal knowledge of the scandals that plagued the chapter, they heard rumors and did nothing about it.[563] Sliwa had plans to form a chapter in Fort Wayne, Indiana's second-largest city. City officials rejected them and believed that a combination of police and Neighborhood Watch programs provided sufficient security.[564]

One of the criticisms of the Guardian Angels was that the background checks were not reliable. Henderson had just joined the Guardian Angels when he led the rape in Gary. It was discovered that he had previously been a member of the Gangster Disciples street gang.[565] Three members of the Indianapolis chapter were forced to leave when their backgrounds could not be verified. Sliwa acknowledged that his records check was probably not as effective as one done by a law enforcement agency.[566]

South Bend started a chapter, but it folded within a year. It lacked public support due to liability issues. Since Guardian Angels is a not-for-profit corporation, it didn't carry insurance. The city could be opened up to lawsuits if there was any official recognition of the Guardian Angels.[567]

The stance of Indianapolis officials toward the Guardian Angels changed from negative to neutral by 1988. Indianapolis hosted the 1987 Pan-American Games, and the police department at least met with the Guardian Angels to see what role they could provide. That was a huge change from just two years earlier.[568]

By 1990, the active membership in the Indianapolis chapter had dwindled to six people. While public officials may not have wanted their services, private companies did. The Gene B. Glick Company requested the Guardian Angels provide security at the Carriage House East Apartments. A low-income apartment complex, it had become a high-crime area beset by drug activity. The violent crime rate for that area had increased by 25 percent from the previous year. The Guardian Angels were given a two-story apartment for their "headquarters" equipped with an office, living area, punching bag and weight bench. Some residents and city officials still questioned their effectiveness.[569]

The Guardian Angels almost returned to Indianapolis after the 2010 shooting at the Black Expo. Today, the Guardian Angels have forty-four chapters in twenty-two states and nineteen countries. The Guardian Angels have expanded into other areas. The Junior Guardian Angels is an early prevention program for children six to fifteen that teaches values and instills a sense of purpose. They have also started the New Guardian Angels Community Block Watch program, similar to the Neighborhood Watch program.[570]

CHAPTER 13

CITIZEN'S ARREST

A citizen's arrest is one of the most misunderstood concepts in our society. People feel that they have the ability to arrest their neighbors for the slightest provocation. The concept of citizen's arrest has dramatically changed since its inception. Some states still have a version of citizen's arrest codified into law; each state is different. Most citizens don't understand the concept of citizen's arrest other than they think they have the power to arrest people. Failing to understand the concept opens a person up to civil and criminal liability, and it can have disastrous consequences.

On February 23, 2020, Ahmaud Arbery was shot and killed while running through the Satilla Shores neighborhood in Glynn County, Georgia. Gregory McMichael and his son, Travis, suspected Arbery of having committed several burglaries in the area. The father and son, armed with a .357-caliber handgun and shotgun, chased Arbery through the neighborhood in their pick-up truck. Their neighbor, William Bryan, followed behind them, recording the incident on his cellphone.

The McMichaels attempted to cut off Arbery as he was running. The vehicle stopped, with Gregory standing in the truck bed and Travis standing outside the driver's door with a shotgun. Arbery attempted to go around the vehicle, where Travis confronted him. There was a struggle between Arbery and Travis that resulted in Arbery being shot by Travis with the shotgun. Gregory had his .357 handgun in his hand but never fired. The McMichaels and Bryan were found guilty on state and federal charges in the killing of Arbery. The McMichaels were sentenced to life imprisonment without parole, while Bryan received life with the possibility of parole after thirty years.

McMichaels' lawyers claimed that they were innocent of any crime based on Georgia law. They were legally carrying their firearms based on Georgia's open-carry law. They also had the right to pursue Arbery and make a citizen's arrest. The law states, "A private person may arrest an offender if the offense is committed in his presence or within his immediate knowledge." Also, under Georgia law, the McMichaels had the right to use deadly force if they felt their lives were in danger.[571]

What is a citizen's arrest? The McMichaels argued that they followed the law when they stopped Arbery. Until May 2021, every state allowed citizen's arrest, although the law's wording differs between states. Traditionally, citizens can make arrests for felonies that are committed in their presence or if they have probable cause to believe that a felony has been committed. The concept dates back to before the country was founded. Before the 1800s, most arrests were of a private nature. Due to a lack of law enforcement, colonists made arrests or paid constables to do it. Some people skipped that step and handed out summary justice on their own.[572]

Urbanization brought major changes as people gave up being their brother's keeper and let formal law enforcement take over. Citizen arrests became rare and were filled with complexities and risks. Law enforcement discourages the practice because it puts civilians in harm's way. Civilians also open themselves up to being civilly liable and/or criminally charged with false imprisonment if they are wrong. Georgia's citizen arrest law dates back to 1863, which allowed white people to capture runaway slaves. After the Arbery case, Governor Brian Kemp signed legislation repealing citizen's arrest, becoming the first state to do so. The new law allows private security or employees of a retail store to detain someone for shoplifting until police arrive or restaurant employees detaining someone for trying to leave without paying.[573]

CITIZEN ARREST IN INDIANA

Under Indiana law, a person may make a citizen's arrest in three ways: if a felony committed in their presence, if they have probable cause to believe that a person has committed a felony or if a misdemeanor involving a breach of the peace is committed in their presence and the arrest is necessary to prevent the continuation of the breach of the peace. In each situation, law enforcement must be notified as soon as practicable.[574]

In the 1950s and '60s, citizens were making arrests for speeding and other minor traffic offenses. At the time, citizen's arrests were only allowed for felonies. Under the Indiana motor vehicle code, only uniformed officers could make arrests for traffic violations. Non-uniformed officers could only make arrests for more serious offenses such as hit-and-runs and driving under the influence. The only exception was that non-uniformed officers could make arrests as long as they were in their jurisdiction.[575]

Citizens did not need to physically restrain someone for it to be an arrest. Local police departments allowed citizens to file affidavits in court attesting to the violation, but it came with a risk. The complainant could be charged with false arrest if the person arrested is later found innocent.[576] Citizen arrests require that law enforcement is called as soon as practicable. The arrests are normally listed as made by the police with citizen assistance. Rarely does a citizen arrest result in a conviction alone.

But that is what happened in 1974 when William Keithley, a municipal court judge, made a citizen's arrest on I-465 in Indianapolis. Donald Cordill was speeding and tailgating the judge's vehicle. The judge changed lanes and then motioned for Cordill to pull over to the side of the road. Keithley approached the vehicle and told Cordill that he was making a citizen's arrest. Cordill was later charged with operating a motor vehicle under the influence, speeding, failure to signal and improper lane usage. Keithley, a former police officer, understood how far the citizen's arrest powers went. He flagged down an Indiana State Police officer to complete the process. Although he was successful at getting a conviction, Keithley discouraged people from making citizen arrests.[577]

Over the years, citizen arrests have been upheld or rejected by the Indiana Supreme Court. In 1972, the court upheld the citizen arrest of a Chicago police officer by two farmers in Newton County. The farmers noticed a suspicious car on their property. As they approached, they found three individuals in possession of marijuana. The officer was convicted, and the court upheld the conviction that a citizen has the right to make an arrest if a felony is committed in their presence.[578] In 1990, the court ruled that a shotgun blast does not constitute a citizen's arrest. Two individuals at a Muncie bar killed another man with a shotgun after he was accused of stealing a woman's wallet. They appealed their murder conviction on the grounds that the judge did not instruct the jury on citizen's arrest. The court upheld the murder conviction and noted that their actions did not follow the citizen's arrest law.[579]

At one time, a citizen's arrest only applied to felonies. But the law was changed to include misdemeanors that constituted a breach of the peace. What exactly constituted a breach of the peace was not entirely clear. In 1996 in Vanderburgh County, Jon Collins pulled over Timothy Hart after he was swerving and crossing the center line. As Hart stopped at a traffic signal, Collins reached through an open window, put the car in park and removed the keys. The police were called, and he was later charged with operating a vehicle while intoxicated.[580]

The trial court granted Hart's motion to suppress the evidence, arguing that the arrest was invalid. The state appealed the ruling, arguing that Collins made a valid arrest under Indiana law. The court overturned the trial court's ruling. The issue was that intoxicated driving was a misdemeanor and whether that could be considered a breach of the peace. Hart argued that his actions did not fit the statutory definition, so the arrest was illegal. The court ruled that driving while intoxicated was a breach of the peace and that the arrest was lawful. The court emphasized that there is risk in making a citizen's arrest, and each person does it at their own peril.[581]

After the case of Ahmaud Arbery, citizen arrest laws have come under scrutiny. Many of these laws are steeped in racism, and citizens can use the power of arrest to intimidate and target people of color. Many citizens are also ignorant of the laws. They don't know the difference between an infraction, misdemeanor or felony or what elements are needed for a crime. They are prone to make mistakes. Finally, citizen arrest can lead to violence, as demonstrated in Arbery's case. Citizen arrests have enormous risks for everyone involved. It is an outdated concept, and arrests should be the responsibility of professional law enforcement officers.

STAND YOUR GROUND LAWS

Stand your ground laws have been linked to a rise in vigilantism that gives what civil rights attorney Ben Crump calls "a virtual get-out-of-jail-free card that is essentially a license to kill."[582] Duty to retreat is a legal requirement in some jurisdictions that states that a threatened person cannot harm someone in self-defense when it is possible to retreat to a place of safety. This is in contrast to the common law principle of the "castle doctrine" that states that a person does not have to retreat if they are in their own home and may use reasonable force, including deadly force, to protect themselves.

In 2005, Florida expanded on the castle doctrine by being the first state to pass the Stand Your Ground law. The law states that "a person who is not engaged in an unlawful activity and who is attacked in any other place where he or she has a right to have no duty to retreat and has the right to stand his or her ground and meet force with force, including deadly force, if he or she reasonably believes it is necessary to do so to prevent death or great bodily harm to himself or herself or another or to prevent the commission of a forcible felony." The castle doctrine was expanded to include anywhere a person has a rightful place to be.[583]

On February 26, 2012, in Sanford, Florida, George Zimmerman, a Neighborhood Watch captain, fatally shot seventeen-year-old Trayvon Martin. Martin was visiting relatives at the time of the shooting. Due to a series of break-ins, Zimmerman became suspicious of Martin and called the police. A confrontation broke out between Zimmerman and Martin. Zimmerman shot and killed Martin, fearing for his life.

The Stand Your Ground law was blamed for the shooting. Although Zimmerman was charged with second-degree murder, a jury acquitted him, claiming that his actions constituted self-defense. The law was criticized because it allows people to kill in public even when they can walk away from danger. There are now over thirty states, Indiana included, with some form of a Stand Your Ground law. Supporters believe that the law help keeps people safe and deters crime.

Critics have nicknamed Stand Your Ground the "shoot first law" and the "right to commit murder law." Critics believe that these laws turn society into the Wild West. While they argue that these laws need to be abolished, prosecutors are beginning to draw a line in the sand as to how far these laws will protect citizens. Missouri was the first state to pass Stand Your Ground laws in the wake of the Trayvon Martin shooting. On April 13, 2023, a white homeowner in Kansas City shot a Black sixteen-year-old, Ralph Yarl. When he was shot, Yarl was picking up his siblings and rang the doorbell at the wrong house. The prosecutor affirmed that standing your ground does not mean that the person has to retreat, but it is also not a blanket defense for shooting someone who approaches with no reasonable fear of being harmed.[584]

Citizen's arrest and Stand Your Ground laws help to justify actions by those who take the law into their own hands. Citizens should familiarize themselves with these concepts before trying to invoke them. Civilians are not law enforcement officers, and they lack the same authority. Taking the law into their own hands or stepping outside of the boundaries of the law could have disastrous consequences for all involved.

CHAPTER 14

FUTURE OF VIGILANTISM

In the twenty-first century, technology has transformed how Americans live their lives. Americans are more easily connected through the use of cellular phones, the Internet and social media apps. Information can be found at the touch of a button. People can form friendships with others worldwide without ever having met in person. Dating websites have replaced the traditional method of courtship. All modes of shopping can be done online, with same-day delivery in many instances. All of this without ever leaving the house. Artificial intelligence, like Siri and Alexa, can answer almost any question, program your lights and tell jokes. There is no doubt that technology makes lives easier.

However, there is concern that some apps encourage vigilantism. On October 26, 2016, the aptly named Vigilante app was released in New York City on the App Store. Designed by Andrew Frame, it showed users where crime was occurring in real time, and it encouraged them to help stop it. The app went viral, and in less than forty-eight hours, Apple pulled the app because of safety concerns.[585] The app was re-released in March 2017 and rebranded as Citizen. The new app dialed down the potential for direct involvement of its users. It would remind users not to approach a crime scene or interfere with an incident. The app would only list calls that threaten public safety, and it eliminated calls dealing with suspicious people, suspicious bags and drug incidents.[586]

Citizen is now available in more than sixty cities, but there is a fear that the app is moving closer to its earlier version. Former employees have stated that the company is not meeting its marketing themes. They fear that the company is heading in a more aggressive direction.[587] In 2021, the Citizen app got a tip that an arsonist set a wildfire in the Los Angeles Pacific Palisades neighborhood. Citizen had just launched a new live-streaming service, OnAir. CEO Frame had hoped to catch the arsonist live on the air. They had a photo of the suspected person, and Frame offered a $30,000 reward for the app user who led to the suspect's arrest. The bounty fueled a city-wide app manhunt. A staffer pointed out that Citizen was violating its own terms of service that prohibited "posting of specific information that could identify parties involved in an incident." LAPD eventually made an arrest, but it was not the suspect that Citizen had identified. People were chasing the wrong person.[588]

VOLUNTEER SLEUTHS

On January 6, 2021, America experienced an attack on democracy when more than 2,000 rioters stormed the U.S. Capitol building to prevent the certification of the Electoral College vote. They believed that President Donald Trump had rightfully won the election and that President Joe Biden had stolen the election. These individuals, many of them far-right extremists and armed militia groups, occupied, vandalized and looted the Capitol. When the dust had settled, 5 people were dead; 4 police officers committed suicide within seven months of the incident. There were hundreds of injuries to rioters and at least 138 police officers, 15 of whom were hospitalized. There have been more than one thousand arrests since the attacks, and the number continues to climb.

Identifying those who participated in the Capitol attacks was a daunting task even for the FBI. Thousands of photos and videos were released by the FBI with the hopes of enlisting the public's help in identifying those individuals. Citizens began to form groups with the mission of identifying those people. They would cross-reference the photos and videos with social media accounts, campaign footage and other publicly available information to determine the identities of the rioters. That information would then be given to the FBI.

These groups go by such names as the Sedition Hunters, Capitol Terrorists Exposers and Deep State Dogs. Regardless of their name, they are part of a large, sprawling social media community spread across the United States united by a common goal: accountability. Like with any new organization, there were some mistakes. Some people were too overenthusiastic and made some false identifications. These groups have now implemented a set of best practices such as not naming people on social media. Publicly identifying people will be left to law enforcement. They are researchers who use the Internet and social media to help fight for justice.[589]

PREDATOR HUNTERS

For as much as technology makes our lives easier, there is a dark side to this technology. Criminals use it to prey on unsuspecting victims. People put their entire lives on the Internet and become easy prey. Billions of dollars are stolen annually from victims through scams and frauds. Criminals use the anonymity of the Internet to further their criminal activities. With cybercrimes being one of the hardest to investigate and prosecute, it has become a favorite tool of cybercriminals. Most of these victims range from the young and educated to the elderly.

Children, the most innocent in society, are also the most vulnerable to cybercriminals. According to the FBI, there are approximately 500,000 sexual predators online; 50 percent of victims are between twelve and fifteen years of age, and online predators contact 89 percent of victims through chat rooms, gaming sites and social media apps. Online sexual predators have created a new crime, sextortion, in which children are convinced to share explicit photos of themselves and are then blackmailed into sending more.[590] While the FBI and local police task forces aggressively investigate these crimes, some in the public feel that law enforcement is not doing enough and are forced to take matters into their own hands.

Predator Catchers Indianapolis (PCI) gained nationwide attention as a group of volunteers that seeks to rid their community of child predators. The founder, Eric Schmutte, founded the group after becoming outraged that sexual predators were not being held accountable amid a lax criminal justice system. As these predators use the computer to prey on children, the group uses it against them. Group members pose as underage children as adults seek to meet them for sexual activities. They lure the child predator into a meeting in public, at which time they expose the person, usually through a live feed on Facebook.[591]

The group has been successful in helping charge a high school music teacher and a Portland, Indiana police officer with child solicitation, among others. While many applaud their efforts, law enforcement agencies consider them vigilantes. Prosecutors in multiple counties have expressed concern that their methods are dangerous. Although they are doing it with the best of intentions, their actions could be detrimental to the successful prosecution of a case.[592]

Some prosecutors are unwilling to charge people based on the activities of these groups. Safety is a major concern, as the group confronts these people in public. If the person was to pull a gun, innocent people could be hurt or killed. There have been times when the group has identified the wrong person, which could lead to a libel or slander lawsuit, not to mention being targeted by angry citizens. There are also ethical considerations. A prosecutor is prohibited from making extrajudicial comments about the videos the group posts online. If a prosecutor takes cases from these groups, the members become agents of the state. Therefore, constitutional safeguards would apply to the subjects pursued by the group.[593]

It is commendable that they want to make a safer world for their children, but everyone needs to know their defined roles.

INDIVIDUAL ACTORS

Some vigilantes choose not to be part of a group but rather act alone. They view themselves as self-appointed crusaders against crime and immorality. The Department of Psychology at the University of Illinois, Champaign–Urbana found that people routinely monitor the activities of others and are eager to punish those who violate laws or societal norms. These individuals take on a vigilante identity. Researchers created the vigilante identity scale (VIS) to assess the degree that people adopt this identity, of which one in five people have a strong endorsement.[594]

The majority of individual vigilantes take on the persona of fictional superheroes. They wear capes and unique disguises, and although they lack superpowers, the media has referred to them as Real Life Super Heroes (RLSH). They are people who adopt the fictional superhero persona in the real world to make the world a better place. While many view them as strange or odd, it doesn't deter them from their mission.[595]

While most prefer to "patrol" independently, they share ideas and network with others. Much like the Avengers, they take on unique names, such as one group in Indianapolis, the Justice Society of Justice. Consisting of two members, Doktor DiscorD and Mr. Silent, they patrol the streets of Indianapolis focusing on deterring violent crime. Mr. Silent wears a black suit with a silver tie and mask, walking the streets of Indianapolis carrying a cane. He said, "I roam the streets of the city looking for those in distress or danger and I do my best to help them. If those in need of help are being mugged or hurt in any way, then you can be assured that I will do something about it. One may ask, how I can call myself a superhero when I can't fly or run at Mach 3. The answer is simple. I am idealistically super. I see what, in my opinion, needs changed in society and I work toward that goal. I can't say if I will ever fight an army of giant robots or a criminal master mind, I just don't know. What I do know, however, is that I will fight injustice in whatever form it takes."[596]

His partner, Docktor DiscorD, wears a black face mask with red and blue bottle cap goggles. When asked what he does, he said, "We don't care about victimless crime like drug use or people buying prostitutes. The kind of CRIME we're talking about is the kind that makes little old ladies afraid to leave their houses."[597] These individual crime fighters do not stay in business long, and Mr. Silent and Doktor DiscorD seem to have retired. But they represent other individuals around the country, like Terrifica in New York patrolling the bar scene and Orlando's Master Legend, who seek to make the world a better place in their own unique way.

ARMED MILITIAS

The history of militias in the United States date back to December 13, 1636, when the Massachusetts Bay Colony general court organized three regiments to defend the colony. This marked the beginning of the organized militia in the United States.[598] Militias in Indiana were first formed in 1807 by Territory Governor William Henry Harrison to protect white settlers from the Native Americans. The Indiana Rangers were divided into three divisions to patrol various routes throughout the state. Each member was required to supply their own horse, ammunition, tomahawk, knives and leather belt.[599]

They disbanded in 1809 but were reactivated in 1811 as the Indiana Territorial Mounted Rangers. They fought at the Battle of Tippecanoe and during the War of 1812 before disbanding for the final time in 1815. During the Civil War, the legislature officially formed the Indiana Legion on

May 11, 1861. It consisted of two divisions of nine brigades numbering ten thousand soldiers. Known as the "Home Guard" or "Minute Men," they fought at the Battle of Corydon and had responsibility for patrolling the state's southern border.[600] During World War I, the Liberty Guard protected the state from German spies and sympathizers. It was renamed the Indiana Guard Reserve (IGR) in 1916, a supplemental military force that assumes the state mission when the Guard is federally mobilized. Today, the Indiana National Guard serves as a component of the U.S. Armed Forces.[601]

Federal and state laws allow the government to form militias to defend the United States or individual states. The problem arises when the government does not authorize them. These unauthorized or private militias usually engage in paramilitary activity using weapons and military techniques. They believe they have the authority to engage in military and law enforcement functions. Group members usually wear military uniforms, tactical gear and/or distinctive insignia.[602]

The January 6 U.S. Capitol attack was an unprecedented attack on democracy. It resulted in five deaths and multiple injuries to rioters and at least 138 police officers, leading to more than one thousand arrests. Many of the rioters were associated with militia-type groups such as the Three Percenters, Proud Boys and the Oath Keepers, all of which are represented in Indiana.[603]

The Three Percenters were founded by Mike Vanderboegh as early as 2008 when he promoted it on his blog. In 2014, he published the movement's doctrine online. The name comes from the claim that only 3 percent of American colonists fought against the British during the American Revolution. They believe that the government is tyrannical and infringes on American's constitutional rights and liberties.[604] In the wake of the Capitol attacks, the national council voted to disband the organization, leaving local groups to carry on the name.[605] The Proud Boys are an extremist group that spews anti-Muslim, misogynistic rhetoric and white nationalist propaganda. Founded by Gavin McInnes, cofounder of *VICE* magazine, in 2016, the group has been designated a terrorist organization by Canada and New Zealand for its role in the Capitol attack.[606]

The Oath Keepers, founded in 2009 by Stewart Rhodes, is one of the largest and most prominent organizations within the militia movement. It formed in the wake of Barack Obama being elected as the first Black president, with their stated purpose being to defend the U.S. Constitution and fight tyranny. The group engages in vigilantism by providing voluntary armed security nationwide at various protests and venues. Members are recruited from the military and law enforcement. The name of the organization derives from the members' vow taken as soldiers or officers to uphold the oath "to support and defend the Constitution against all enemies, foreign and domestic."[607]

More than a dozen members took part in the Capitol attacks. They were charged with conspiracy for planning to obstruct an official proceeding by interfering with the certification of the Electoral College vote. The group's founder, Rhodes, and eleven other members were indicted for seditious conspiracy.[608] On May 23, 2023, Rhodes was sentenced to eighteen years in prison, the longest sentence to date of anyone who participated in the attack.[609]

In the wake of the Capitol attack, the remaining board members renamed themselves Oath Keepers USA to dissociate themselves from the previous organization. While they do not consider themselves a militia, they support the rights of those who do. The Oath Keepers consider themselves a "Constitutional Service Organization." Their objectives remain the same, but members are expected not to be associated with any group or activity that seeks to discriminate or overthrow the government.[610]

In 2019, the Southern Poverty Law Center identified 576 anti-government groups, of which 181 were militia groups. Although the number represents a steep decline from the 1,360 groups at the end of Obama's first term, they still pose a concern for the democracy of the United States.[611]

NOTES

Introduction

1. Matthew Impelli, "New York City's Most Dangerous Year of Crime Compared to 2022: Analysis," *Newsweek*, October 10, 2022.
2. Douglas Linder, "The Trial of Bernhard Goetz: An Account," Famous Trials, https://www.famous-trials.com/goetz/133-home.
3. History, "Boston Tea Party," https://www.history.com/topics/american-revolution/boston-tea-party.
4. History, "Shays' Rebellion," https://www.history.com/topics/early-us/shays-rebellion#section_7.
5. Merriam-Webster, "Vigilante," https://www.merriam-webster.com/dictionary/vigilante.
6. H. Rosenbaum and P. Sedberg, *Vigilante Politics* (Philadelphia: University of Pennsylvania Press, 1976).
7. G. Marx and D. Archer, "The Urban Vigilante," *Psychology Today* (January 1976): 45–50.
8. D. Lim, "Revenge, Our Cinematic Tradition," *Los Angeles Times*, October 19, 2009.
9. J. Keller, "Anti-Government Unrest and American Vigilantism," *The Atlantic*, https://www.theatlantic.com/politics/archive/2010/03/anti-government-unrest-and-american-vigilantism/38229.
10. L. Johnston, "What Is Vigilantism?," *British Journal of Criminology* (1996).

11. Rafael Carranza, "Border Vigilantes, and the Wall They Might Be Watching," *USAToday*, https://www.usatoday.com/border-wall/story/vigilante-militia-patrol-us-mexico-border/559753001.
12. WNYC Studios, "Neighborhood Watch Members React to George Zimmerman Verdict," July 16, 2013, https://www.wnycstudios.org/podcasts/takeaway/segments/306918-neighborhood-watch-members-weigh.
13. National Neighborhood Watch, "About," https://www.nnw.org/about-national-neigborhood-watch.
14. Department of Criminal Justice, Indiana University, https://criminaljustice.indiana.edu/about/history.html.

Chapter 1

15. J. Obert and E. Mattiacci, "Keeping Vigil: The Emergence of Vigilance Committees in Pre–Civil War America," *Perspectives on Politics* 16, no. 3 (2018).
16. Historical Society of Pennsylvania, "Vigilant Committee and the Underground Railroad," https://www.portal.hsp.org/unit-plan-items/unit-plan-51.
17. D. Warner, "Anti-Corruption Crusade or 'Businessman's Revolution'?," *California Legal History* 6 (2011).
18. History, "The Railroad Police," http://www.therailroadpolice.com/history.
19. R. Smith, "From the Ohio to the Mississippi: A Story of a Railroad," Railroads of Cincinnati, 1965, http://cincyrails.com/files/FromTheOhioToTheMississippi.pdf.
20. HistoryNet, "Reno Gang's Reign of Terror," https://www.historynet.com/reno-gangs-reign-of-terror/?f.
21. "Buried Treasure," *The Republic*, August 25, 2002.
22. Legends of America, "Reno Gang & the 1st Big Train Robbery," https://www.legendsofamerica.com/we-renogang.
23. PBS, "Allen Pinkerton's Detective Agency," https://www.pbs.org/wgbh/americanexperience/features/james-agency.
24. "Famous Detective Cases," *Appleton City Journal*, June 25, 1925.
25. Ibid.
26. "Lynch Law in Indiana," *Aegis Intelligencer*, December 25, 1868.
27. "News," *Seymour Weekly Democrat*, December 23, 1868.

28. "Lynch Law in Indiana."
29. "Train Robbing as a Profession Was Started in Indiana by Reno Family," *Indianapolis Star*, December 31, 2017.
30. "Reno Gang Earliest to Be Lynched," *Evansville Courier*, December 29, 1900.
31. "The New Albany Lynching and Hanging," *Newcastle Weekly Courant*, January 1, 1869.
32. "Lynch Law in Indiana."
33. Ibid.
34. Ibid.
35. "The New Albany Tragedy," *Evansville Daily Journal*, December 16, 1868.
36. "Lynch Law in Indiana."
37. "From Indianapolis," *Fort Wayne Daily Gazette*, May 1, 1869.
38. "Famous Detective Cases," *Appleton City Journal*, June 25, 1925.

Chapter 2

39. Andrew Hind, "The Knights of the Golden Circle," *History Magazine* (October/Nov 2011).
40. Ibid.
41. "Knights of the Golden Circle Brought to Mind," *Indianapolis News*, July 2, 1904.
42. "Astounding Developments Before the U.S. Grand Jury," *Evansville Daily Journal*, August 6, 1862.
43. "Knights of the Golden Circle Brought to Mind."
44. "Astounding Developments Before the U.S. Grand Jury."
45. Ibid.
46. "Golden Circle Conspiracy," *Indianapolis Journal*, September 4, 1892.
47. "Knights of the Golden Circle Brought to Mind."
48. "News," *Indianapolis Journal*, May 26, 1902.
49. "Testimony of a Double Traitor," *Seymour Times*, November 17, 1864.
50. "Knights of the Golden Circle Brought to Mind."
51. "Golden Circle Conspiracy."
52. "Andrew Humphreys and the Order of General Hovey," *Jasper Weekly Courier*, January 7, 1865.
53. "Knights of the Golden Circle Brought to Mind."
54. "The Golden Circle," *South Bend Tribune*, December 7, 1897.

55. Encyclopedia Britannica, "Ex-Parte Milligan," https://www.britannica.com/event/Ex-Parte-Milligan.
56. "The Milligan Suit," *Evansville Journal*, May 18, 1871.
57. "A Celebrated Case," *Muncie Morning News*, November 3, 1885.
58. "Poor Stephen Horsey," *Princeton Clarion Leader*, November 18, 1897.
59. "Organizer of Sons of Liberty Is Dead," *Indianapolis News*, June 7, 1906.
60. "Milligan Is Dead," *Fort Wayne Sentinel*, December 21, 1899.

Chapter 3

61. "The White Cap Outrages," *Indianapolis Journal*, August 19, 1888.
62. "The Attorney-General's Account," *Indianapolis Journal*, August 19, 1888.
63. "Mob Rule by the Lash," *The Sun*, October 14, 1888.
64. "Origin of White Caps," *Ann Arbor Argus*, January 20, 1893.
65. "Story of the White Caps," *Indianapolis News*, August 23, 1893.
66. "Lynch Law in Indiana," *Indianapolis Journal*, September 26, 1887.
67. "White-capism in Indiana," *Indianapolis Journal*, February 10, 1892.
68. "Mob Rule by the Lash."
69. Ibid.
70. "History of Whitecaps," *Bremen Enquirer*, September 1, 1893.
71. "A Detective's Story of the Organization," *Indianapolis Journal*, August 19, 1888.
72. "History of Whitecaps."
73. "The Indiana White Caps," *Indiana State Sentinel*, January 2, 1889.
74. "Mob Rule by the Lash."
75. "State Items," *Evansville Daily Journal*, November 17, 1871.
76. "From Hoosierdom," *Daily Democrat*, July 1, 1891.
77. "Lynch Law in Indiana."
78. "The White Caps," *Edinburgh Daily Courier*, September 13, 1888
79. "Mob Rule by the Lash."
80. "The Conrads' Deadly Guns," *Indianapolis Journal*, August 7, 1893.
81. "The White Caps Again," *Indianapolis News*, August 25, 1893.
82. "Four Men Murdered," *Muncie Evening Press*, August 7, 1893.
83. Ibid.
84. "Brave Brothers," *Daily Democrat*, August 8, 1893.
85. Ibid.

86. "Another Trial Fiasco," *Indianapolis Journal*, April 17, 1898.
87. "An Unwelcome Letter," *The Republic*, March 21, 1892.
88. "Left Her Husband to His Fate," *Daily Democrat*, October 27, 1892.
89. "Legislative Notes," *Dearborn County Register*, February 14, 1889.
90. "Can't Convict White Caps," *Rushville Republican*, October 17, 1889.
91. "Taken from Bed Whipped by Mob," *Huntington Herald*, May 6, 1911.
92. "First Whitecapper Under Conviction," *Richmond Item*, February 1, 1912.
93. "Old Alibi Dead," *Bedford Daily Mail*, February 9, 1912.
94. "Whitecapping Case Reported," *The Times*, June 23, 1928.

Chapter 4

95. Remley Herr, "Horse Stealing: The Crime that Was," Robert T. Ramsay Jr. Archival Center of Wabash College.
96. *Indian Affairs: Law and Treaties* (Washington, D.C.: Government Printing Office, 1904).
97. Herr, "Horse Stealing."
98. "The Horse-Thief Captor," *Indianapolis News*, May 16, 1894.
99. "When the Minute Men Rode in Indiana," *Indianapolis Star*, August 8, 1965.
100. "Horse-Thief Captor."
101. Ibid.
102. M.H. Mott, *History of the Regulators of Northern Indiana* (N.p.: Indiana Journal Company, 1859).
103. Ibid.
104. Ibid.
105. "The Hanging of Gregory McDougle by the Indiana Regulators," *Garrett Clipper*, September 17, 1914.
106. "Northern Indiana Regulators," *Steuben Republican*, December 23, 1914.
107. "Old Time Regulators Organize," *Muncie Daily Times*, April 17, 1896.
108. "Law and Order Society," *Indianapolis Journal*, October 5, 1897.
109. "Farmers Plan War on Rural Robbers," *Indianapolis Star*, October 8, 1907.
110. "Law and Order Society."
111. "To Have Rival," *Rushville Republican*, September 29, 1906.
112. "To Stop Auto Scorching," *Indianapolis News*, May 31, 1906.

113. "Plan to Fight Auto Bandits," *Richmond Item*, October 2, 1923.
114. Wabash College, "A Bill Concerning Detective Associations," 1907, https://palni.contentdm.oclc.org/digital/collection/p15705coll34/id/2144/rec/1.
115. "Defect Reported in Bill," *Indianapolis News*, February 24, 1925.
116. "May Change Horse Thief Sleuth Law," *The Times*, January 7, 1925.
117. "Clashes Feature Primary Election of Party Leaders," *Indianapolis Star*, May 6, 1925.
118. "Ruling on Power of Horse Thief Detectives," *Noblesville Ledger*, May 12, 1925.
119. "Apology Frees Police Captain," *Indianapolis Times*, December 22, 1925.
120. "Seek to Learn Status of Horse Thief Detectives," *Indianapolis News*, June 5, 1926.
121. "Horse Thief Detectives," *Indianapolis News*, October 5, 1927.
122. Digital Civil Rights Museum, Ball State University, "Resurgence of the KKK in Indiana," https://www.digitalresearch.bsu.edu/digitalcivilrightsmuseum/items/show/112.
123. "Mrs. Daily Douglas Barr Heard at Klan Meetings," *Star Press*, September 4, 1923.
124. Karen Abbott, "Murder Wasn't Very Pretty: The Rise and Fall of D.C. Stephenson," *Smithsonian Magazine*, https://www.smithsonianmag.com/history/murder-wasnt-very-pretty-the-rise-and-fall-of-dc-stephenson-18935042.
125. "'I Am the Law!' Boasted Stephenson, Now Convict," *Palladium-Item*, August 10, 1927.
126. "Legislators' Move for Impeachment of Jackson Meets Vigorous Opposition," *Indianapolis Times*, February 18, 1928.
127. "Horse Thiefers One Branch of Klan That's Dead," *Evansville Press*, November 11, 1926.
128. "Horse Thief Detectives Shorn of Their Powers," *Daily Reporter*, November 24, 1926.
129. "Gilliom Hears Four in Klan Ouster Suit," *Indianapolis Star*, March 7, 1928.
130. "Group Disavows Link with Klan," *South Bend Tribune*, June 11, 1929.
131. "Association Drops Horsethief Title," *The Times*, October 5, 1928.
132. "Senate Engages in Discussion on Klan, Religion," *Evansville Courier*, March 1, 1929.
133. "Votes to Cut Out Horse Thief Law," *Indianapolis Star*, March 7, 1933.

Chapter 5

134. "Roots: The Lynches of Galway," *Irish America Magazine* (July 2017), https://www.irishamerica.com/2017/05/roots-the-lynches-of-galway.
135. "Lynch Law," *Baraboo Republic*, January 30, 1889.
136. Ibid.
137. Ibid.
138. NAACP, "History of Lynching in America," https://naacp.org/find-resources/history-explained/history-lynching-america.
139. Equal Justice Initiative, "Lynching in America: Confronting the Legacy of Racial Terror," 2017, https://lynchinginamerica.eji.org/report.
140. "Lynching and Law," *Indianapolis Journal*, October 24, 1887.
141. "Public Meeting," *Political Beacon*, May 4, 1839.
142. "We Understand," *Political Beacon*, May 3, 1839.
143. "Lynching and Law," *Indianapolis Journal*, October 24, 1887.
144. "History of the Levi Gang," *Evansville Journal*, September 20, 1897.
145. Ibid.
146. "Five Burglars," *Brookville Democrat*, September 23, 1897.
147. Ibid.
148. Ibid.
149. Ibid.
150. Ibid.
151. Ibid.
152. "The Leader," *Brookville Democrat*, September 23, 1897.
153. "Recalls Lynching in Ripley County," *Indianapolis Star*, April 30, 1911.
154. "Hex Hughes Is Not Guilty," *Indianapolis News*, March 1, 1898.
155. "Indiana Lynching," *Huntingburgh Argus*, December 30, 1898.
156. "Cause of Lynching," *Indianapolis Journal*, December 26, 1898.
157. "Could Have Saved Him," *Indianapolis Journal*, December 31, 1898.
158. "Old Hoosier Lynchings," *Indianapolis Journal*, January 8, 1899
159. "Anti-Lynching Bill Killed," *Indianapolis News*, January 28, 1899.
160. "News," *Jackson County Banner*, November 30, 1899.
161. "News," *Daily Mail*, April 13, 1899.
162. "Anti-Lynching Law," *Bedford Democrat*, March 24, 1899.
163. "Mob Law," *Booneville Standard*, December 21, 1900.
164. "Another Lynching," *Indianapolis News*, December 18, 1900.
165. "Gov. Mount Was Warned," *Princeton Clarion-Leader*, December 27, 1900.

166. "The Sullivan County Lynching," *Indianapolis Journal*, November 22, 1902.
167. "Brought to Bay Was the Brute," *Muncie Evening Press*, November 20, 1902.
168. "After a Sheriff," *The Herald*, December 5, 1902.
169. "Decided for Sheriff Dudley," *Huntington Herald*, November 21, 1903.
170. "Sheriff Removal in Lynchings," *Indianapolis News*, January 6, 1905.
171. "Lynching Versus Law," *Fort Wayne Sentinel*, March 29, 1902.
172. "Indiana's Fair Name," *Palladium-Item*, June 7, 1904.
173. "Will Seek Repeal of the Death Penalty," *Star Press*, December 17, 1904.
174. Peter Granitz, "Senate Passes Anti-Lynching Bill and Sends Federal Hate Crime Legislation to Biden," NPR, March 8, 2022, https://www.npr.org/2022/03/08/1085094040/senate-passes-anti-lynching-bill-and-sends-federal-hate-crimes-legislation-to-bi.
175. "Out in Indiana," *Indianapolis News*, October 5, 1897.

Chapter 6

176. "War and Sabotage Spawn Vigilante Group," *Colombian*, January 10, 1957.
177. "Black Tom Ruins Still in Flames," *Brooklyn Daily Eagle*, July 31, 1916.
178. Saladin Ambar, "Woodrow Wilson: Domestic Affairs," University of Virginia, 2023, https://millercenter.org/president/wilson/domestic-affairs.
179. "East Germantown Signs Gone for Repair; Name of Town Same," *Palladium-Item*, July 19, 1959.
180. Pressbooks. "The United States Prepares for War," University of Hawaii, https://pressbooks-dev.oer.hawaii.edu/ushistory/chapter/the-united-states-prepares-for-war.
181. Office of the Director of National Intelligence, "The Espionage Act of 1917," https://www.intelligence.gov/evolution-of-espionage/world-war-1/america-declares-war/espionage-act.
182. "President Signs Espionage Bill, Making It Law," *Bridgeport Times and Evening Farmer*, June 16, 1917.
183. "200,000 U.S. Secret Agents Cover Nation," *Chicago Tribune*, August 25, 1917.
184. "'Get Slacker' League Formed," *Evansville Press*, August 18, 1917.

185. "Tar and Feather IWW Workers," *Brazil Daily Times*, February 13, 1918.
186. "Gregory Takes Blame in Raids," *Indianapolis Star*, September 12, 1918.
187. Gregory S. Rose, "The Distribution of Indiana's Ethnic and Racial Minorities in 1850," *Indiana Magazine of History* 87, no. 3, https://www.jstor.org/stable/27791487.
188. "The Teaching of German," *Indianapolis News*, April 5, 1901.
189. "State's Organic Laws Blamed for Dilemma," *Star Press*, January 14, 1918.
190. "F.C. Miller Petitions Under Law," *The Times*, December 3, 1917.
191. "Hot Mayoralty Race on Again at Michigan City," *South Bend News-Times*, January 12, 1917.
192. "Indiana City May Have Three Mayors Monday," *The Republic*, January 4, 1918.
193. "Miller in Office as Michigan City Mayor," *South Bend Tribune*, January 7, 1918.
194. "State News Items," *Bedford Daily Mail*, January 7, 1918.
195. "Sedition Bill in Wilson's Hands," *Evansville Courier*, May 8, 1918.
196. "Debs Indicted for Speech," *Evansville Courier*, July 1, 1918.
197. "Red-Blooded Americans Refuse to Allow Disloyal Utterances," *The Times*, April 9, 1918.
198. "New Order to Be Instituted," *Princeton Daily Clarion*, June 22, 1918.
199. "A.P.L. with 250,000 Member, Quits Feb. 1," *The Times*, December 27, 1918.
200. "New Anti-German Bill Is Passed," *The Times*, February 18, 1919.
201. "Exit the German Dachshund," *Jasper Weekly Courier*, August 23, 1918.

Chapter 7

202. "Bank Cashier Killed by Foiled Robbers," *Star Press*, June 15, 1919.
203. "Bandits Wife Won't Get Reward," *The Times*, October 21, 1920.
204. "Rest of Bank Bandits Taken to Crown Point," *The Times*, July 2, 1919.
205. "Tolleston Bank Robbery Is Cleaned Up Today," *The Times*, June 28, 1919.
206. "The Parole Abuse," *South Bend Tribune*, July 5, 1919.
207. "Quick Justice Meted to Murderous Gang," *Idaho Daily Statesman*, July 4, 1919.
208. "Sheriff Hurries Off with His Prisoner," *Star Press*, July 20, 1919.

209. "Senator McCray to Appear for Men Sentenced to Die," *Garrett Clipper*, September 25, 1919.
210. "Life Sentences for 4 Slayers," *Richmond Item*, October 2, 1920.
211. "Hearing Set on State Police Bill," *Seymour (IN) Tribune*, February 2, 1921.
212. "State Police Bill," *Evansville Courier*, February 4, 1921.
213. "Plan Formation of State Police," *Star Press*, December 26, 1920.
214. FDIC, "Historical Timeline," https://www.fdic.gov/about/history/timeline/1900-1919.html.
215. Paul Musgrave, "A Primitive Method of Enforcing the Law," *Indiana Magazine of History* (September 2006).
216. FBI, "The FBI and the American Gangster, 1924–1938," https://www.fbi.gov/history/brief-history/the-fbi-and-the-american-gangster.
217. "5 Million Stolen in Iowa in 3 Years," *Gazette*, August 21, 1923.
218. Forba McDaniel, "The Vigilantes Check Crime," *American Bankers Association Journal* 19 (1926).
219. "2 Bank Robbers Get 10–20 Years," *Evansville Courier* and Press, November 24, 1923.
220. "Cashier Killed by Bank Robbers," *Seymour (IN) Tribune*, November 8, 1923.
221. "Admit Murder of Cashier, Report," *Daily Republican*, November 9, 1923.
222. "Feeling Runs High After Prisoner Confesses Slaying," *Indianapolis Star*, November 10, 1923.
223. "Given Life Sentence for Killing Cashier of Edwardsport Bank," *Evansville Courier* and Express, January 15, 1924.
224. "Will Be Sentenced for Killing Cashier," *Star Press*, March 2, 1924.
225. "The Bandit Business," *Palladium-Item*, January 1, 1925.
226. "Bankers' Committee Completes Draft of State Police Bill," *Palladium-Item*, December 30, 1924.
227. "State Police," *Indianapolis News*, November 25, 1924.
228. "State Police Bill to Die," *Indianapolis Star*, February 22, 1925.
229. PATrooper, "History," http://www.patrooper.com/history.html.
230. "Broaden Powers for Governor," *Indianapolis Star*, March 3, 1925.
231. "Wants Death Penalty for Bandits," *Tri-County Banner*, January 30, 1925.
232. "Overdoing the Penalty," *Indianapolis Star*, February 11, 1925.
233. "Death Penalty Removed from Bank Banditry Bill," *Indianapolis Star*, February 12, 1925.
234. "12 Banks Robbed in 2 Months," *The Times*, May 28, 1925.

235. "Drastic Action Is Plan of Shank," *Indianapolis News*, June 11, 1925.
236. "Governor Is Much Perturbed," *The Times*, June 10, 1925.
237. Ibid.
238. "Move to Make Bank Robbery Bad Business," *The Republic*, June 12, 1925.
239. "Advises Bankers to Exterminate Bandits," *Indianapolis News*, June 11, 1925.
240. "Citizens' Vigilant Committees Urged by Iowa Banker," *Indianapolis Star*, March 19, 1924.
241. "Iowa Bank Robberies Few," *Sioux City Journal*, May 4, 1922.
242. "Citizens' Vigilant Committees Urged by Iowa Banker."
243. "Bankers of the State to Start on Campaign to Stop Bank Robberies," *Woodford County Journal*, March 19, 1925.
244. "Bank Robberies in Illinois Fall Off 62 Per Cent," *St. Louis-Globe Democrat*, November 5, 1925.
245. "More Deputies to Be Named to Thwart Bank Robberies," *St. Louis Post-Dispatch*, November 14, 1924.
246. "The Bandit Business," *Palladium-Item*, January 1, 192; "County Unit Protective Plan Proves Effective," *Palladium-Item*, June 12, 1928.
247. "Move to Make Bank Robbery Bad Business," *The Republic*, June 12, 1925.
248. "Local Bankers Hear Plans for Their Defense," *Noblesville Ledger*, November 23, 1925.
249. "Mayor Shank Declares War on Indianapolis Bank Bandits; Order Given—'Shoot to Kill,'" *Indianapolis Star*, June 12, 1925.
250. "Vigilantes Hit Target Center in State Shoot," *The Republic*, June 24, 1926.
251. "Operators to Play Part of 'Paul Revere,'" *The Republic*, November 23, 1925.
252. "Bank Attacks Less Since Adoption of Vigilante System," *Palladium-Item*, June 19, 1926.
253. "112 Banks Favor Bureau for Crime," *Indianapolis News*, December 16, 1926.
254. "Advice from the National Crime Commission," *Star Tribune*, September 8, 1926.
255. "Small Town Police Force Placed on Par with the City Detective Bureau," *Daily Republican*, August 6, 1927.
256. "Eight Robberies Are Committed in Last 9 Days," *Rushville Republican*, December 23, 1930.

257. "Five Clinton Robbers Named as Kidnappers," *Call-Leader*, May 15, 1931.
258. "Death Sentence for Trio Asked," *Indianapolis Star*, December 18, 1930.
259. "Dead Bank Bandit Has Been Identified," *Rushville Republican*, December 19, 1930.
260. "America's Worst Outlaw," *The Times*, September 19, 1931.
261. "Mike McCormick: A Quiet 1930 Morning in Clinton," *Terre Haute Tribune-Star*, May 25, 2019.
262. "Two Clinton Bank Bandits Kill Selves," *Palladium-Item*, December 16, 1930.
263. "Third Clinton Robber Dies of Posse's Shots," *The Republic*, December 18, 1930.
264. "Death Sentence for Trio Asked," *Indianapolis Star*, December 18, 1930.
265. "2 in Clinton Bank Job Get Life Terms," *Indianapolis Star*, January 4, 1931.
266. "America's Worst Outlaw," *The Times*, September 19, 1931.
267. "Holdup Suspects Plead Not Guilty," *Indianapolis Star*, December 24, 1930.
268. "Bank Banditry Is Unprofitable," *Muncie Evening Press*, May 13, 1932.
269. "Court Holds Stolen Bonds Must Be Paid," *Noblesville Ledger*, October 17, 1935.
270. FBI, "History," https://www.fbi.gov/history/timeline.
271. Indiana State Police, "How We Began," https://www.in.gov/isp/about-isp/history/how-we-began.
272. "Banker Vigilantes Will Be on Alert for Any Saboteurs," *Star Press*, December 19, 1941.

Chapter 8

273. "There Is Room to Improve Local Governments," *South Bend Tribune*, September 2, 1999.
274. "Constable Fees," *Indianapolis News*, March 12, 1924.
275. Ibid.
276. "Haughville a Court of Extortion," *Indianapolis News*, May 4, 1907.
277. "Probe Bares Extortion by Constables," *Indianapolis Times*, April 15, 1931.
278. "Ruling Aimed at Constables," *The Times*, October 12, 1939.

279. Officer Down Memorial Page, "Constable Robert Murphy," https://www.odmp.org/officer/20459-constable-robert-murphy.
280. "Town Marshals," *Indianapolis News*, March 22, 1907.
281. Officer Down Memorial Page, "Deputy Marshal George Carney," https://www.odmp.org/officer/22358-deputy-marshal-george-carney.
282. North Carolina Sheriffs Association, "History of the Sheriff," https://ncsheriffs.org/about/history-of-the-sheriff.
283. Roger Scott, "ROOTS: A Historical Perspective of the Office of Sheriff," National Sheriff's Association, https://www.sheriffs.org/about-nsa/history/roots.
284. NRA, "The Grouseland Rifle: A Longrifle by John Small," November 2, 2016, https://www.americanrifleman.org/content/the-grouseland-rifle-a-longrifle-by-john-small 1.
285. Scott, "ROOTS."
286. Officer Down Memorial Page, "William Gresham," https://www.odmp.org/officer/18958-sheriff-william-gresham.
287. Encyclopedia of Indianapolis, "Indianapolis Metropolitan Police Department," https://indyencyclopedia.org/indianapolis-metropolitan-police-department-impd.
288. "Attention Battalion," *Indianapolis News*, February 12, 1875.
289. "Interest in Police System Repeal Plank," *Indianapolis News*, August 8, 1904.
290. Ibid.
291. "A Lucky Administration," *Indianapolis Journal*, August 26, 1891.
292. "Interest in Police System Repeal Plank," *Indianapolis News*, August 8, 1904.
293. "Merit System Study Is Made," *Indianapolis Star*, March 17, 1935.
294. "Forced Retirement Irks 41 Year Police Veteran," *Evansville Courier* and Press, November 28, 1958.
295. "Academy to Train, Accredit Law Enforcement Officers," *Star Press*, November 17, 1968.
296. "State Police Academy Plans Move Forward with Board's Establishment," *Reporter-Times*, June 30, 1967.
297. "99 Hoosier Policemen to Graduate Saturday," *The Herald*, July 31, 1969.
298. Indiana Law Enforcement Academy, "Historical Overview," https://www.in.gov/ilea/about-the-academy/historical-overview.
299. "Watching through the Night," *Indianapolis Journal*, November 28, 1886.

300. "The Merchant Policemen," *Indianapolis Journal*, March 24, 1889.
301. "Won't Wear Uniforms," *Indianapolis Journal*, June 7, 1900.

Chapter 9

302. Police1, "An Overview of the Federal Police Force," https://www.police1.com/how-to-become-a-police-officer/articles/an-overview-of-the-federal-police-force-3lUfL7uRZ5zjdWbT.
303. Frederick S. Calhoun, *The Lawmen: United States Marshals and Their Deputies, 1789–1989* (Washington, D.C.: Smithsonian Institution Press, 1990).
304. U.S. Marshal Service, "List of US Marshals—Indiana," https://www.usmarshals.gov/sites/default/files/media/document/list-of-us-marshals-indiana.pdf.
305. "Historic Little Town of Vernon Still Holds Spotlight in Indiana," *Indianapolis Star*, January 21, 1940.
306. Norman Ansley, "The United States Secret Service—An Administrative History," *Journal of Criminal Law and Criminology* 47, no. 1 (1956).
307. "Life of Major Rathbone," *Journal News*, April 20, 1926.
308. "Pete McCartney," *Times-Picayune*, June 14, 1890.
309. "Pete McCartney Dead," *Monroeville Breeze*, October 23, 1890.
310. "Tried to Kill a Detective," *Indianapolis Journal*, October 31, 1887.
311. "Died in Prison," *Green Bay Press-Gazette*, October 23, 1890.
312. "The King of Coniakers," *Indianapolis Journal*, October 30, 1887.
313. "Pete McCartney," *Richmond Item*, July 7, 1887.
314. "King of Coniakers."
315. "Pete McCartney," June 14, 1890.
316. "Death of Constable Welch," *Evansville Daily Journal*, April 15, 1862.
317. Indiana Archives and Records Administration, "Miles Ogle."
318. "Pinkerton and the Renos," *Daily Mail*, February 9, 1895.
319. "He Made Green Goods," *Evansville Journal*, July 28, 1893.
320. "Criminal News," *Chicago Tribune*, January 10, 1877.
321. "Heavy Sentence of a Counterfeiter," *Rutland Daily Herald*, March 20, 1877.
322. "Miles Ogle," *Public Ledger*, January 14, 1885.
323. "Counterfeiting," *Knoxville Daily Journal*, March 15, 1885.
324. "Miles Ogle," *Daily Memphis Avalanche*, January 20, 1885.
325. "Miles Ogle Guilty," *Cincinnati Enquirer*, December 14, 1890.

326. "Miles Ogle Dead," *Commercial Appeal*, June 27, 1900.
327. "Secret Service Covered by Veil," *South Bend Tribune*, December 21, 1908.
328. "Limits Secret Service," *Indianapolis News*, May 2, 1908.
329. John F. Fox, "The Birth of the Federal Bureau of Investigation," FBI, 2003, https://www.fbi.gov/history/history-publications-reports/the-birth-of-the-federal-bureau-of-investigation.
330. "White Slave Probe," *New York Tribune*, January 4, 1910.
331. "Traffic Is Proved by Purchase of the Girls," *Press and Sun Bulletin*, April 30, 1910.
332. "Rockefeller, Jr., Offers Much Coin," *Brazil Daily Times*, February 8, 1910.
333. "Railroad Company Has Issued Order," *The Republic*, October 31, 1910.
334. "White Slave Bill Passed by Senate," *Washington Times*, June 25, 1910.
335. "White Slave Law Is Being Enforced," *South Bend Tribune*, October 29, 1910.
336. "Sharp Watch Kept on Huerta's Moves by Special Agents," *Brooklyn Daily Eagle*, July 4, 1915.
337. "Bureau of Investigation to Be Opened in the City," *Indianapolis News*, June 2, 1914.
338. "Continue Probe of Price Rise," *Huntington Herald*, August 19, 1914.
339. "State-Wide Inquiry," *Cincinnati Enquirer*, August 19, 1914.
340. "Mayor Myatt Is Reelected," *Quad-City Times*, March 30, 1915.
341. "Ramsey Succeeds Kearney," *Indianapolis News*, November 20, 1914.
342. "United States Taking a Hand," *Columbus Republican*, December 31, 1914.
343. "Federal Investigator Quits," *Indianapolis Star*, November 15, 1916.
344. "Lack of System," *Fort Wayne Daily News*, June 4, 1917.
345. "Protect State from Railing Hyphenates," *Evansville Courier*, July 19, 1917.
346. "Call to Battle Thrills Capital," *The Republic*, May 19, 1917.
347. "How the Draft Law Reaches Men Who Failed to Register," *The Times*, December 6, 1917.
348. "Classed as Deserters," *Indianapolis News*, September 27, 1917.
349. "U.S. Will Ask Death Penalty," *Bedford Daily Mail*, August 7, 1917.
350. "Draft List Stolen," *Fort Wayne Daily News*, August 2, 1917.
351. "Demands Suppression of 'Finished Mystery,'" *Indianapolis News*, March 15, 1918.

352. "5,000 Books Turned In to Federal Agent," *Star Press*, March 20, 1918.
353. "E.L. Osborne Recommended for Good Job," *Journal and Courier*, October 5, 1921.
354. "Colored Barber Begins Working for Uncle Sam," *Indiana Daily Times*, January 9, 1922.
355. FBI, "The FBI and the American Gangster, 1924–1938," https://www.fbi.gov/history/brief-history/the-fbi-and-the-american-gangster.
356. "U.S. Offices Merged," *Indianapolis Times*, November 29, 1929.
357. "Osborne Named Head of Bureau," *Journal and Courier*, November 20, 1929.
358. "Omaha Branch Office," Nebraska State Journal, June 9, 1934.
359. "Crack U.S Agent Assigned to City," *Indianapolis Star*, May 24, 1934.
360. "New Head for Capital Office," *The Republic*, September 8, 1934.
361. "Murder Charge Placed Against G-man Slayer," *Richmond Item*, August 18, 1935.
362. "Nelson's Pal Gets Life for Murder of Federal Agent," *St. Louis Post-Dispatch*, March 26, 1935.
363. "Is First Man to Be Hanged Under New US Statute," *The Times*, March 24, 1936.
364. Dawn Mitchell, "A History of Executions in Indiana," IndyStar, https://www.indystar.com/story/news/2019/12/11/indiana-executions-full-list-people-executed-since-1897/4357164002.
365. "Hanging Revival," *Indianapolis Times*, February 10, 1936.
366. Jane Hedeen, "The Road to Prohibition in Indiana," Indiana Historical Society.
367. "The Haskin Daily Letter," *South Bend Tribune*, December 16, 1919.
368. "Federal Director for Prohibition Law," *Daily Republican*, January 16, 1920; "South Bend May Hold Dry Office," *South Bend Tribune*, May 12, 1921.
369. "Home Made Wines and Cider Banned Orbison Asserts," *Huntington Press*, February 21, 1920.
370. "Congress Is Asked to Amend Dry Law," *Fort Wayne Sentinel*, January 22, 1920.
371. CDC, "1918 Pandemic," https://www.cdc.gov/flu/pandemic-resources/1918-pandemic-h1n1.html.
372. "No Whiskey for Influenza in State Is Edict," *Muncie Evening Press*, January 30, 1920.
373. "Thirty-Eight Government Operatives Arrive and Make Wholesale Arrests in South Bend," *South Bend Tribune*, June 24, 1920.

374. "158 Given Whiskey on Orbison Notes Revealed by Files," *Indiana Daily Times*, January 13, 1921.
375. "Orbison Got 3 Quarts Whiskey for His 'Work,'" *Indiana Daily Times*, January 17, 1921.
376. "Decision by Judge W.M. Sparks Cited," *Rushville Republican*, January 17, 1921.
377. "158 Given Whiskey."
378. "In Prohibition Work," *Indianapolis News*, July 5, 1921.
379. "U.S. Loses No Time on the Job," *The Times*, April 17, 1923.
380. Officer Down Memorial Page, "Robert G. Anderson," https://www.odmp.org/officer/1219-warehouse-agent-robert-g-anderson.
381. "Politics and Prohibition," *Indianapolis Times*, September 21, 1925.
382. "Complete Shakeup of Dry Officials Begins in Indiana," *Indianapolis Star*, September 20, 1925.
383. "House Agrees to Enforcement Plan of the President," *Richmond Item*, May 20, 1930.
384. "Says Dry Laws to Be Enforced," *Indianapolis Star*, August 12, 1933.
385. PBS Frontline, "A Social History of America's Most Popular Drugs," https://www.pbs.org/wgbh/pages/frontline/shows/drugs/buyers/socialhistory.html.
386. Donald Richter, "Richter: When Sears Sold Cocaine," *Commercial News*, January 12, 2020, https://www.commercial-news.com/community/richter-when-sears-sold-cocaine/article_18040136-33bf-11ea-a4f4-fb8171cc1262.html.
387. "Blame Placed on Physicians," *Waterloo Press*, January 2, 1913.
388. "Some Good, Some Bad," *Boonville Standard*, April 4, 1913.
389. "'Dope' Officer Named for State of Indiana," *Star Press*, March 12, 1915.
390. "Senate Has Opportunity to Hit 'Dope' with Porter Bill," *San Francisco Examiner*, April 11, 1930.
391. "The Marijuana Menace," *The Times*, March 3, 1937.
392. Officer Down Memorial Page, "Mansel Burrell," https://www.odmp.org/officer/2575-special-agent-mansel-ross-burrell.

Chapter 10

393. New England Historical Society, "When Massachusetts Abolished the State Police," https://newenglandhistoricalsociety.com/when-massachusetts-abolished-the-state-police.

394. Connecticut State Police Museum, "A Brief History of the Connecticut State Police," http://www.cspmuseum.org/CMSLite/?CMSLite_Page=7.
395. Explore PA History, "Behind the Marker," https://explorepahistory.com/hmarker.php?markerId=1-A-2D1.
396. Pennsylvania State Police HEMC, "Pennsylvania State Police," https://www.psp-hemc.org/history/psp.html.
397. "Moyca Newell Dies, Helped Establish N.Y. State Cops," *Central New Jersey Home News*, February 26, 1968.
398. "State Police Department," Bedford *Daily Democrat*, December 24, 1920.
399. "Score of Indiana Mayors Hostile to State Police Bill," *Fort Wayne Sentinel*, February 17, 1919.
400. "State Police Bill Is Killed in the House," *Muncie Evening Press*, February 20, 1919.
401. "State Police Bill Hearing," *Star Press*, February 1, 1921.
402. Connie Zeigler, "Street Railway Strikes," Encyclopedia of Indianapolis, https://indyencyclopedia.org/street-railway-strikes.
403. "Strike and Riot," *Jackson County Banner*, November 5, 1913.
404. "Police Are Sympathetic," *Rushville Republican*, November 5, 1913.
405. "They Resigned When Outvoted," *Rushville Republican*, November 25, 1913.
406. "Forces Shank to Step Down," *Evening Star*, November 29, 1913.
407. "Nation's Crime Wave Laid to Bad Liquor and War," *Courier-Journal*, December 29, 1920.
408. "State Police Department," Bedford *Daily Democrat*, December 24, 1920.
409. Ibid.
410. "State Police Bill Subject of Hot Debate," *Indiana Daily Times*, February 4, 1921.
411. Gary Public Library and Jennifer Guiliano, "The Steel Strike of 1919 in Gary," Discover Indiana, https://publichistory.iupui.edu/items/show/603.
412. "State Police Bill Subject of Hot Debate."
413. "Hearing Set on State Police Bill."
414. "Cost of Recent Strike Service," *Evening Star*, November 19, 1913.
415. "State Police Efficiency," *Indianapolis News*, December 21, 1920.
416. "Plan Formation of State Police," *Star Press*, December 26, 1920.
417. "State Police Department," *Bedford Daily Democrat*, December 24, 1920.

418. "Deputy Sheriff Bill Approved," *Indianapolis Star*, February 18, 1921.
419. "Trend of Legislation," *Evansville Courier*, February 6, 1921.
420. "Hearing Set on State Police Bill."
421. "Session Closed," *Monticello Herald*, March 10, 1921.
422. "New Automobile Law," *Journal and Courier*, August 20, 1921.
423. "State Constabulary Need Urged in Report," *Indianapolis News*, December 29, 1921.
424. "Brief State News," *Bedford Daily Mail*, May 9, 1921.
425. "Local Man Heads New Department," *Rushville Republican*, June 1, 1921.
426. "New Automobile Law," *Journal and Courier*, August 20, 1921.
427. "Plan Formation of State Police," *Star Press*, December 26, 1920.
428. "Recover 118 Cars Last Half of 1921," *Daily Republican*, February 24, 1922.
429. "Automobile Association Asks Credit for State Certificate of Title Law," *Star Press*, November 12, 1922.
430. "Police Bill Knocked Out 32–14, by Vote in Senate," *Indianapolis Star*, February 20, 1923.
431. "State Police Bill to Be Presented by Marion Senator," *Indianapolis Star*, January 17, 1923.
432. "Police Bill Knocked Out 32–14."
433. "Trend of Legislation," *Evansville Courier*, February 6, 1921.
434. "State Police System Favored for Indiana," *South Bend Tribune*, December 5, 1924.
435. "Bankers Committee Completes Draft of State Police Bill," *Palladium-Item*, December 30, 1924.
436. "State Police Bill Opposition Heard," *Indianapolis Star*, January 12, 1925.
437. "Makes Plea for Help in Efforts to Enforce New Laws of State," *Franklin Evening Star*, May 5, 1925.
438. "Slump in Auto Deaths Fails to Show Up Here," *Indianapolis Times*, June 22, 1925.
439. "Checking Speeders," *Evansville Journal*, March 21, 1925.
440. "Stronger Liquor Law Aim of Dry Forces," *Indianapolis News*, November 8, 1924.
441. "Frank L. Mather Talks on Police over WSBT," *South Bend Tribune*, February 18, 1926.
442. "Presents Good Arguments for State Police," *Urbana Daily Courier*, January 7, 1922.

443. "Martin Favors Establishing State Police," *Quad-City Times*, March 11, 1926.
444. "Better Defective than Not at All," *Star Press*, May 28, 1927.
445. National Library of Medicine, "Alphonse Bertillion," https://www.nlm.nih.gov/exhibition/visibleproofs/galleries/biographies/bertillon.html.
446. "How Criminals Are Identified," *Star Tribune*, January 14, 1901.
447. "The Bertillion System," *Indianapolis Journal*, May 30, 1897.
448. "Criminals," *Evansville Journal*, November 24, 1897.
449. "First Bertillion Case," *Indianapolis Journal*, April 8, 1898.
450. "Work of Police Would Improve," *Daily Republican*, May 5, 1915.
451. National Library of Medicine, "Juan Vucetich," https://www.nlm.nih.gov/exhibition/visibleproofs/galleries/biographies/vucetich.html.
452. "Fingerprints of Twins Declared to Be Not Alike," *Indianapolis Times*, March 18, 1927.
453. "William West and Will West; Not Same Man," *Leavenworth Times*, April 10, 1907.
454. "Indiana Bankers Want Bureau of Identification," *Garrett Clipper*, September 23, 1926.
455. "Fingerprints of Criminals Will Be Made," *Reporter Times*, August 6, 1927.
456. "New Bureau to Open," *Indianapolis News*, June 30, 1927.
457. "Indiana Turning from Petting of Criminals," *Garrett Clipper*, May 12, 1927.
458. "New State Bureau to Function Soon," *The Times*, June 3, 1927.
459. "Same Place, Same Cast in '27 Stickup," *Kokomo Tribune*, December 8, 1955.
460. "Indiana Bankers Want Bureau of Identification," *Garrett Clipper*, September 23, 1926.
461. "Same Place, Same Cast in '27 Stickup."
462. "Frank Badgley Serving Time at Michigan City," *Reporter Times*, October 27, 1927.
463. "Lee, Original Wooden Pistol Maker," *Indianapolis Star*, March 11, 1934.
464. "Robber Erred in Picking His Town," *Daily Republican*, October 10, 1927.
465. "Bank Bandit Sent to Penitentiary for Life," *Rushville Republican*, October 14, 1927.
466. Officer Down Memorial Page, "Patrolman John J. Gerka, Jr.," https://www.odmp.org/officer/5391-patrolman-john-j-gerka-jr.

467. "Brown and Badgley Die Calmly for Killing Hammond Policeman," *Indianapolis News*, February 23, 1949.
468. Gregory Myers, "Newton's County Only State Governor Immortalized with Historical Marker," *Newton County Enterprise*, June 10, 2019, https://www.newsbug.info/newton_county_enterprise/news/local/newton-countys-only-state-governor-immortalized-with-historical-marker/article.
469. "Retro Indy: KKK in Indiana and Their Leader, D.C. Stephenson," *IndyStar*, February 20, 2014, https://www.indystar.com/story/news/history/retroindy/2014/02/20/d-c-stephenson/5641029.
470. "Officials Rap Idea of Police Army in State," *Indianapolis Times*, December 21, 1928.
471. "Niblack Sets State Police Quality Mark," *Indianapolis Times*, December 18, 1928.
472. "Shift in State Police Rule Is Holmes' Plea," *Indianapolis Times*, February 5, 1929.
473. "Bill Bans Use of State Police on Voting Days," *Indianapolis Times*, February 22, 1929.
474. "Plans to Place State Police on Military Basis," *Indianapolis Star*, December 8, 1928.
475. "Officials Rap Idea of Police Army in State."
476. "Leslie Loses in Fight Against Party Chiefs," *Huntington Press*, February 17 1929.
477. "See State Police Bill as Bone of Contention," *The Times*, February 23, 1929.
478. "State Police Bill Changes Approved," *Indianapolis Star*, February 16, 1929.
479. "Auto Fund State Police Bill Hit," *Argos Reflector*, February 14, 1929.
480. "See Political Significance in Conference," *The Times*, October 14, 1929.
481. "State Public Safety Bill Lands in Senate," *Indianapolis News*, February 13, 1931.
482. "New Officers of State Go into Office," *Rushville Republican*, December 1, 1930.
483. "Entirely New State Police Force Planned," *Richmond Item*, November 30, 1930.
484. "Efficient State Police," *Boonville Standard*, April 4, 1930.
485. "State Police," *Richmond Item*, June 22, 1932.
486. "Abolish the State Police," *The Times*, May 12, 1932.

487. "State Police Manipulation," *Indianapolis Star*, November 21, 1932.
488. "State Public Safety Department Proposed," *Indianapolis Star*, July 22, 1932.
489. "Power of State Police Widened; M'Nutt Controls," *Indianapolis Star*, March 1, 1933.
490. Ibid.
491. "State-Wide Police Radio System," *Hancock Democrat*, July 20, 1933.

Chapter 11

492. American Experience, PBS, "John Dillinger," https://www.pbs.org/wgbh/americanexperience/features/dillinger-john-dillinger.
493. "New Carlisle Bankers Tied Up Bandits," *News-Messenger*, June 21, 1933.
494. "Bandits Sought at Logansport," *Star Press*, August 17, 1933.
495. "Test to Be Made on Dillinger Gun," *Indianapolis News*, September 23, 1933.
496. "Nab Prisoner in House Raid; Pistols Found," *Dayton Daily News*, September 22, 1933.
497. "Dillinger Is Under Guard in Lima Jail," *Dayton Daily News*, September 29, 1933.
498. "Ten Convicts in State Prison Escape, Still at Large; Find Kidnaped Sheriff Unharmed," *Star Press*, September 27, 1933.
499. "State Militia Ordered Out in Search for Convicts," *The Times*, September 28, 1933.
500. "Personnel Changes Seen as Prison Escape Factor," *Richmond Item*, September 28, 1933.
501. "Dillinger's Arrest in Dayton Was Planned So Well He Didn't Have a Chance?" *Dayton Daily News*, July 23, 1934.
502. "Bank Robbery Loot $14,993," *Daily Advocate*, October 9, 1933.
503. "Three Shoot Down Officer, Lock Up 2; Flee with Outlaw," *Indianapolis Star*, October 13, 1933.
504. "3 Loot Auburn Police Arsenal," *Indianapolis Star*, October 16, 1933.
505. "Dillinger Is Identified as Leader of Bandits in Arsenal Raid at Peru," *Muncie Evening Press*, October 21, 1933.
506. "Desperados Rob Western State Bank of $5000," *Logansport Pharos-Tribune*, October 24, 1933.
507. "Indiana Cops Unite to Nab Bank Robbers," *Newark Advocate*, October 26, 1933.

508. "Desperado Eludes Police Trap after Running Gun Fight," *Post-Crescent*, November 16, 1933.
509. "Name Three Convicts as Bank Bandits," *Wisconsin State Journal*, November 21, 1933.
510. "Dillinger Gang Member Taken Back to Prison," *Evansville Journal*, November 20, 1933.
511. "Another Chicago Detective Is Slain," *Journal Gazette*, December 15, 1933.
512. "Bullet Intended for Gangster Hits State Policeman," *Indianapolis Star*, December 21, 1933.
513. "Murder of O'Malley Is Widely Deplored," *The Times*, January 16, 1934.
514. "Tucson Police Chief Praises Work of Men," *Muncie Evening Press*, January 26, 1934.
515. "Governor Ready to Extradite," *The Times*, January 26, 1934.
516. "Police Remove Dillinger from Arizona by Plane," *St. Louis Post-Dispatch*, January 30, 1934.
517. "'He's Safe Here,' Says Mrs. Holley," *Indianapolis News*, January 31, 1934.
518. "Toy Pistol Fashioned from Old Washboard," *The Times*, March 5, 1934.
519. "Enemy No. 1," *Cincinnati Enquirer*, May 20, 1934.
520. "Six Bandits Rob Bank in South Dakota," *The Item*, March 6, 1934.
521. "St. Paul Mob or Dillinger Gang Blamed in Raid," *Globe-Gazette*, March 14, 1934.
522. "Dillinger Is Responsible for Bank Raid," *Hinton Daily News*, May 4, 1934.
523."Dillinger in Robbery Today," *Daily Reporter*, June 30, 1934.
524. "Doctor Gives Clue to Bank Robber Gang," *News-Herald*, July 2, 1934.
525. FBI, "John Dillinger," https://www.fbi.gov/history/famous-cases/john-dillinger.

Chapter 12

526. Kevin Baker, "'Welcome to Fear City'—the Inside Story of New York's Civil War, 40 Years On," *Guardian*, https://www.theguardian.com/cities/2015/may/18/welcome-to-fear-city-the-inside-story-of-new-yorks-civil-war-40-years-on.

527. Research and Destroy New York City, "Welcome to Fear City," pamphlet, https://researchdestroy.com/welcome-to-fear-city.pdf.
528. "Benevolent Angel or Opportunistic Devil?" *Poughkeepsie Journal*, December 27, 1987.
529. "Foiling Rape, These 3 Were Magnificent," *New York Daily News*, April 19, 1979.
530. "'Angels' Declare War on Muggers," Courier Post, September 5, 1979.
531. Ibid.
532. "B'klyn Bus Riders Have 'Angels' Looking Over Them," *New York Daily News*, October 26, 1979.
533. "Where Angels Tread," *Herald Statesman*, December 7, 1980.
534. Ibid.
535. "Spread of Angel Patrols Worries Some," *Great Falls Tribune*, August 17, 1981.
536. "Angels Start Rights Rally to Capital," *Daily Register*, January 8, 1982.
537. "Spread of Angel Patrols Worries Some."
538. "Foiling Rape, These 3 Were Magnificent."
539. "Gary Mayor's Bid for Fifth Term Challenged," *South Bend Tribune*, May 2, 1983.
540. "Crime Key Campaign Issue," *Munster (IN) Times*, April 29, 1983.
541. "Guardian Angels Eye Gary," *The Times*, April 28, 1983.
542. "Angels to Train City Unit," *Indianapolis News*, July 28, 1983.
543. "Guardian Angels Get Warm Welcome in Gary," *Journal and Courier*, May 25, 1983.
544. Ibid.
545. "Heat Exhaustion Mars Angels Patrol in Gary," *The Times*, July 29, 1983.
546. "Police Will Wait, See on Angels," *The Times*, May 25, 1983.
547. "Guardian Angels Eye Hammond," *The Times*, July 29, 1983.
548. "First Class of Guardian Angels Graduates Tonight," *The Times*, October 13, 1983.
549. "Guardian Angels' Patrol Starts in E.C," *The Times*, November 29, 1984.
550. "Look Homeward Angels," *Indianapolis News*, December 1, 1983.
551. "Guardian Angels Plan to Watch Over the City," *Indianapolis Star*, June 5, 1983.
552. "Sliwa Says City Could Be Model," *Indianapolis Star*, December 16, 1983.
553. "Angels' Leadership Problems Not New," *The Times*, April 2, 1984.

554. "Guardian Angels Patrol Circle City but Manage to Break Up Few Crimes," *Journal and Courier*, October 1, 1984.
555. "'Angels' to Patrol Columbia Center," *The Times*, December 19, 1983.
556. "Ex-Angel Boss Led a Dual Life, Probe Reveals," *The Times*, April 2, 1984.
557. "Weapons Bust," *The Times*, April 2, 1984.
558. "Lake County Sheriff Targeted in Gun Probe," *Seymour (IN) Tribune*, May 9, 1984.
559. "Lake County Sheriff Indicted on Corruption Charges," Associated Press, March 4, 1985, https://apnews.com/article/2dfd46236e27a41fed9f86c300d48332.
560. "'Angel' to Get 3 Years," *Indianapolis News*, July 21, 1984.
561. "2 Rapists Sentenced," *The Times*, June 15, 1984.
562. "Ex-Angel Leader Gets 20 Years," *The Times*, June 22, 1984.
563. "Shake-Up Ordered in Gary Guardian Angels," *Vidette Messenger of Porter County*, April 7, 1984.
564. "Fort Wayne Officials Shun Help of Guardian Angels," *Evansville Courier*, November 1, 1984.
565. "2 Gary Men Convicted by Jury," *The Times*, June 15, 1984.
566. "Angels' Leadership Problems Not New."
567. "Guardian Angels 'On Their Own,'" *South Bend Tribune*, February 20, 1989.
568. "Angels, IPD Will Discuss Games Plan," *Daily Journal*, July 30, 1987.
569. "Angels Spread Wings Over Apartments," *Indianapolis News*, July 3, 1992.
570. Guardian Angels, http://guardianangels.org.

Chapter 13

571. Richard Fausset, "What We Know About the Shooting Death of Ahmaud Arbery," *New York Times*, August 8, 2022.
572. "Citizen Arrest Becomes Rare Due to Hazards," *Anderson Daily Bulletin*, March 18, 1976.
573. Ashish Valentine, "What Is the Citizen's Arrest Law at the Heart of the Trial Over Ahmaud Arbery's Death?," NPR, October 26, 2021.
574. Indiana Code Title 35, Criminal Law and Procedure, 35-33-1-4.
575. "Court Rules Driver Guilty of Speeding," *South Bend Tribune*, December 8, 1959.

576. "Speeders Facing Citizen Arrest," *The Republic*, September 13, 1960.
577. "Judge Makes Citizen Arrest; Suspect Convicted," *Indianapolis Star*, September 17, 1974.
578. "State Supreme Court Upholds Newton Citizens Arrest Case," *Journal and Courier*, June 9, 1972.
579. "Court: Shotgun Blast Is Not Citizen's Arrest," *Reporter-Times*, September 14, 1990.
580. "Appeals Court Rules Citizen's Arrest Valid," *South Bend Tribune*, July 31, 1996.
581. *State v. Hart* (1996).
582. Curtis Anderson and Lindsay Whitehurst, "Stand Your Ground Laws Proliferate after Trayvon Spotlight," PBS, https://www.pbs.org/newshour/nation/stand-your-ground-laws-proliferate-after-trayvon-spotlight.
583. National Conference of State Legislatures, "Self-Defense and 'Stand Your Ground,'" March 1, 2023, https://www.ncsl.org/civil-and-criminal-justice/self-defense-and-stand-your-ground.
584. Adeel Hassan, "What Are 'Stand Your Ground' Laws, and When Do They Apply?," *New York Times*, April 19, 2023.

Chapter 14

585. Avery Hartmans, "The Controversial App for Avoiding Crime in Your Area Is Back in the App Store, and It's Now Called 'Citizen,'" *Insider*, March 14, 2017.
586. Sarah Perez, "Banned Crime Reporting App Vigilante Returns as Citizen, Says Its 'Report Incident' Feature Will Be Pulled," *Tech Crunch*, March 10, 2017.
587. David Ingram and Cyrus Farivar, "Inside Citizen: The Public Safety App Pushing Surveillance Boundaries," *NBC News*, June 2, 2021.
588. Joseph Cox and Jason Koebler, "'Find This Fuck': Inside Citizen's Dangerous Effort to Cash In on Vigilantism," *VICE*, May 27, 2021.
589. S. Murray, "Meet the Internet Sleuths Tracking Down the January 6 Insurrectionists," *CNN*, June 11, 2021, https://www.cnn.com/2021/06/11/politics/internet-sleuths-january-6-insurrectionists/index.html.
590. Patrick Nelson, "Deep Dive: FBI Estimates 500,000 Online Predators Are a Daily Threat to Kids Going Online," KOAA News, https://www.

koaa.com/news/deep-dive/fbi-estimates-500-000-online-predators-are-a-daily-threat-to-kids-going-online.

591. Holly Hays, "These Civilians Hunt Child Predators. Expert Warns They're 'Playing with Fire,'" *USAToday*, February 25, 2021, https://www.usatoday.com/story/news/nation/2021/02/25/indianapolis-predator-catchers-hunt-offenders-experts-urge-caution/4549340001.
592. Dustin Grove, "Vigilante Justice: Online Groups Target Child Predators, Indiana Prosecutors Concerned About 'Risky Behavior,'" WTHR, https://www.wthr.com/article/news/investigations/13-investigates/vigilante-justice-online-groups-target-child-predators-indiana-prosecutors-predator-catchers-indianapolis/531-056f5a21-cb50-42b3-bc85-fb6eae459c3e.
593. Max Lewis, "Delaware County Prosecutor Blasts Recent Predator Catcher Group Confrontation," Fox59 News, October 26, 2022, https://fox59.com/indiana-news/delaware-county-prosecutor-blasts-recent-predator-catcher-group-confrontation.
594. Diana Yates, "Vigilantism Is an Identity for Some People, Researchers Report," University of Illinois, March 22, 2022, https://psychology.illinois.edu/news/2022-03-22/vigilantism-identity-some-people-researchers-report.
595. Real Life Super Heroes, https://www.rlsh.net/index.html.
596. RLSH, "Mr. Silent," https://wiki.rlsh.net/wiki/Mr._Silent.
597. RLSH, "Doktor DiscorD," https://wiki.rlsh.net/wiki/Doktor_DiscorD.
598. National Guard, "National Guard Birth Date," https://www.nationalguard.mil/about-the-guard/how-we-began.
599. Indiana's Historic Pathways, "Rangers," 2023, https://buffalotrace.indianashistoricpathways.org/index.php/rangers.
600. "Credits Indiana Legion with Good Work during Civil War," *Indianapolis Star*, March 2, 1910.
601. Indiana National Guard, "History of the Indiana National Guard," https://www.in.gov/indiana-national-guard/about/history-and-museums.
602. Georgetown University, "Fact Sheet: Unlawful Militias in Indiana," Institute for Constitutional Advocacy and Protection, https://www.law.georgetown.edu/icap/wp-content/uploads/sites/32/2020/09/Indiana.pdf.
603. Ryan Martin and Tim Evans, "Indiana's Militia Wave Is 'Disturbingly Similar' to Past Fringe Group Activity," *IndyStar*, January 28, 2021.

604. Southern Poverty Law Center, "Three Percenters," https://www.splcenter.org/fighting-hate/extremist-files/group/three-percenters.
605. The Three Percenters Original, TTPO's Final Statement, February 21, 2021, thethreepercenters.org.
606. Southern Poverty Law Center, "Proud Boys," https://www.splcenter.org/fighting-hate/extremist-files/group/proud-boys.
607. Southern Poverty Law Center, "Oath Keepers," https://www.splcenter.org/fighting-hate/extremist-files/group/oath-keepers.
608. Ibid.
609. Cary Johnson, "Stewart Rhodes, Oath Keepers Founder, Sentenced to 18 Years for Seditious Conspiracy," NPR, May 25, 2023, https://www.npr.org/2023/05/25/1178116193/stewart-rhodes-oath-keepers-verdict.
610. Oath Keepers USA, https://usaoathkeepers.com.
611. Niall McCarthy, "The Evolution of Anti-Government Extremist Groups in the U.S.," *Forbes* (2021), https://www.forbes.com/sites/niallmccarthy/2021/01/18/the-evolution-of-anti-government-extremist-groups-in-the-us-infographic/?sh=307b78944e45.

ABOUT THE AUTHOR

Robert Bowling is a retired police officer and local historian. He is the author of *Wicked Fishers* and a contributing author to *Celebrating Hamilton County, Indiana, 200 Years of Change*. With a passion for honoring fallen police officers, he serves as a historical researcher for the "Officer Down Memorial Page" and an ambassador to the National Law Enforcement Officer Memorial Fund. He is a contributing writer to *Officer Magazine*, focusing on law enforcement history. His other works have been featured in the *Michigan History Magazine*, *National Pastime* and *Journal of School Safety*. He currently serves as the historian for the Fishers Historical Society and as a member of the Police History Society based in London, England.